# THE DAILY STUDY BIBLE

(OLD Testament)

General Editor: John C. L. Gibson

## GENESIS

Volume 1

# GENESIS

## Volume 1

JOHN C. L. GIBSON

WESTMINSTER JOHN KNOX PRESS
LOUISVILLE, KENTUCKY

Published by
The Saint Andrew Press
Edinburgh, Scotland
and
Westminster John Knox Press
Louisville, Kentucky

PRINTED IN THE UNITED STATES OF AMERICA

11  13  15  17  16  14  12

ISBN (Great Britain) 0 7152 0465 3

3    4    5    6    7    8

**Library of Congress Cataloging in Publication Data**

Gibson, John C. L.
  Genesis.

  (The Daily study Bible series)
  Bibliography: p.
  1. Bible. O.T. Genesis—Commentaries. I. Title. II. Series:
Daily study Bible series (Westminster Press)
BS1235.3.G53   1981          222'.11077          81-7477
                                                  AACR2

ISBN (U.S.A.) 0-664-21801-6 (v. 1)
ISBN (U.S.A.) 0-664-24568-4 (pbk. : v. 1)

# GENERAL PREFACE

This series of commentaries on the Old Testament, of which my own volume on *Genesis* 1-11 is one of the first, has been planned as a companion series to the much-acclaimed New Testament series of the late Professor William Barclay. As with that series, each volume is arranged in successive headed portions suitable for daily study. The Biblical text followed is that of the Revised Standard Version or Common Bible. Eleven contributors share the work, each being responsible for from one to three volumes. The series is issued in the hope that it will do for the Old Testament what Professor Barclay's series succeeded so splendidly in doing for the New Testament— make it come alive for the Christian believer in the twentieth century.

Its two-fold aim is the same as his. Firstly, it is intended to introduce the reader to some of the more important results and fascinating insights of modern Old Testament scholarship. Most of the contributors are already established experts in the field with many publications to their credit. Some are younger scholars who have yet to make their names but who in my judgment as General Editor are now ready to be tested. I can assure those who use these commentaries that they are in the hands of competent teachers who know what is of real consequence in their subject and are able to present it in a form that will appeal to the general public.

The primary purpose of the series, however, is *not* an academic one. Professor Barclay summed it up for his New Testament series in the words of Richard of Chichester's prayer—to enable men and women "to know Jesus Christ more clearly, to love Him more dearly, and to follow Him more nearly." In the case of the Old Testament we have to be a little more circumspect than that. The Old Testament was completed long before the time of Our Lord, and it was (as it still is) the sole Bible of the Jews, God's first people, before it became part of the Christian Bible. We must take this fact seriously.

Yet in its strangely compelling way, sometimes dimly and sometimes directly, sometimes charmingly and sometimes embarrassingly, it holds up before us the things of Christ. It should not be forgotten that Jesus Himself was raised on this Book, that He based His whole ministry on what it says, and that He approached His death with its words on His lips. Christian men and women have in this ancient collection of Jewish writings a uniquely illuminating avenue not only into the will and purposes of God the Father, but into the mind and heart of Him who is named God's Son, who was Himself born a Jew but went on through the Cross and Resurrection to become the Saviour of the world. Read reverently and imaginatively the Old Testament can become a living and relevant force in their everyday lives.

It is the prayer of myself and my colleagues that this series may be used by its readers and blessed by God to that end.

New College
Edinburgh

JOHN C.L. GIBSON
General Editor

# CONTENTS

## ILLUSTRATIONS

# INTRODUCTION

THE NAME

The name Genesis, meaning "origin", goes back to the ancient Greek translation of the Old Testament. In the Hebrew Bible the book is called *Bereshith* after its opening phrase "In the beginning". It is the first of the five books of the *Torah* or "Law". A term sometimes applied by Greek-speaking Jews to the Torah was *pentateuchos,* which is an adjective meaning "(the book) consisting of five books". From this comes the modern name Pentateuch used by scholars. The fuller title of the Authorized and the Revised Standard Versions, "The first book of Moses (commonly) called Genesis", is no older than Luther's German Bible, though it reflects an ancient tradition of the Jews that the whole Torah had been written by Moses. This tradition was current in New Testament times (see for example Luke 24:27), but it is not found in the Old Testament itself. The book of Genesis is therefore strictly speaking anonymous.

THE "AUTHOR"

According to the scholars our present Genesis has been made up out of three major documents or written sources, to which they assign the labels "J", "E", and "P". Each of these "hands" had its distinctive style, which can sometimes be recognized even in English translation. And each had its own special interests or slant. But none of them points us to an author in any full sense. Rather the men responsible for the documents should be regarded as collectors and "re-tellers" of older traditions which had been brought to Palestine by the Hebrew tribes. The original "genius" of the book is the people of Israel itself. Or to be a little more exact, it is the unknown "bards" or professional "singers of tales" who during the Wilderness Wandering and in the period of the Judges first gave literary shape to the memories and experiences and the hopes and fears of the newly born nation. The work of these "singers of tales"

was entirely oral and has disappeared, but if any one deserves
the title of Genesis' "author", it is they.

It follows from what has just been said that Genesis is
essentially a folk literature. The vast bulk of it consists of
stories which still carry about them the marks of having been
composed to entertain and to instruct ordinary folks. We have
to remember this all the time as we study it. It is *not* addressed
to sophisticated modern people like ourselves who have lost the
taste for simple story-telling, and who do our theology in a
philosophical way. It knows nothing about abstract doctrines
or about the findings of modern science, and it ought not to
have questions put to it which presuppose such matters. We are
much more likely to get through to its message if we try in our
imaginations to stand alongside its first Hebrew audiences and
listen to it with their ears. God is speaking to us in Genesis, but
we must be humble enough to realize that he is not speaking
directly to us, but only to us *through them*. We may wish later
to restate the message in terms that make it more relevant for
our generation. That is only as it should be. But there is no
doubt where we must start.

ITS TWO PARTS

There is a definite break in the book at the end of Chapter 11.
The stories before that concern the creation of the world and the
pre-history of humankind. Their canvas is the universe and
their subject God's dealings with the whole human race. The
stories from Chapter 12 onwards concern a single man Abraham and his family and descendants. Their canvas is the tiny
land of Canaan and its immediate vicinity and their subject is
God's dealings with his special people. The present volume
restricts itself to Chapters 1–11. Because these chapters have
always been in the centre of controversy about the Bible, it will
go into the literary and theological issues at considerable
length. A second volume will be devoted to Chapters 12–50,

which are more straightforward and where a less detailed treatment of such issues will suffice.

THE CONTENTS OF CHAPTERS 1–11

These may be briefly set out as follows:

| | |
|---|---|
| 1:1–2:4(a) | The story of Creation |
| 2:4(b)–3:24 | The story of the Garden of Eden |
| 4:1–16 | The story of Cain and Abel |
| 4:17–5:32 | Genealogies of Cain and Seth |
| 6:1–4 | The story of the Angel-marriages and the Nephilim (giants) |
| 6:5–9:19 | The story of the Flood |
| 9:20–28 | The story of the curse on Canaan |
| 10:1-32 | Genealogy of the sons of Noah |
| 11:1–9 | The story of the Tower of Babel |
| 11:10–32 | Another genealogy of Shem and the genealogy of Terah, the father of Abraham |

The story of the Angel-marriages and the Nephilim in 6:1–4 is a mere scrap, and there are other fragments of stories embedded in the genealogies—about some of the descendants of Cain, particularly Lamech, in 4:17ff., about Seth in 4:25-26, about Enoch in 5:21–24, about Lamech the father of Noah in 5:28–31, about Nimrod in 10:8ff., and about Terah in 11:26–32. There must have been fuller stories in existence in early Israel about these primaeval heroes, but we are not given them.

THE PURPOSE OF CHAPTERS 1–11

Behind these chapters lies a large body of traditions about how the Hebrews conceived the beginning of the world and the rise of the nations and of human civilization in the remote period before history proper began. From this cycle of stories a few were selected by the "authors" of the documents "P" and "J" ("E" does not come in till after Chapter 12) to provide a background to the history of their own race as God's chosen people.

These stories relate how God created this world as a good place, but how human beings in their sin have ruined it. Sin is set forth as disobedience of God, but chiefly as rebellion, as humanity trying to usurp God's role in governing the world. The effects of this rebellion are luridly portrayed. The picture is an exceptionally sombre one and the view of "man" is deeply pessimistic. But we are not allowed to forget that God is in charge, and that he is containing the situation from utter collapse against the time when he will take positive action to reclaim the Kingdom that is properly his. The scene is being set for the call to Abraham at the beginning of Chapter 12, to the Jews the first father of the chosen race, to the Christians the first skirmisher in a long warfare between the forces of good and of evil which did not end until God sent his own Son to earth to win the decisive battle through his Cross and Resurrection.

But in Genesis that victory is still far in the future. In these chapters we have invaluable teaching about God's creation of the world and about his providence over nature and in the march of events, but the abiding impression they leave is of a violent and benighted humanity not realizing its desperate need of salvation. They tell us that we belong to that humanity, and that unless we are willing to go through the terrible experience of being flung out of Paradise with Adam, we can never hope to be with our Saviour in Paradise Regained.

# GENESIS

## THE STORY OF CREATION

Genesis 1:1–2:4(a)

Genesis Chapter 1 (with its continuation in the first few verses of Chapter 2) is one of the immortal documents of the religious spirit. It has that strange mixture of simplicity and profundity which is the mark of all great literature. We shall be going on in this commentary to analyse it verse by verse and sometimes word by word in order to try (we can do no more) to fathom some of its depths. But first let us read it over as a whole, let us listen to its sonorous and craggy phrases, let us admire the masterly architecture of its design, and above all let us drink in the stark simplicity of its central message.

## THE SOVEREIGNTY OF GOD

Genesis 1:1–2:4(a) (*cont'd*)

### (i)

That message is the *sovereignty of God*. Because he created the world it belongs to him and he decides everything that happens in it. Certainly, if we go by other references to Creation in the Old Testament, few lessons come through more strongly than that. Here is a selection of these references from the two books where they occur most frequently.

*Firstly* from the Psalms:

> The earth is the Lord's and the fulness thereof,
>    the world and those who dwell therein;
> for he has founded it upon the seas,
>    and established it upon the rivers.

(Ps. 24:1–2)

> The heavens are thine, the earth also is thine;
>    the world and all that is in it, thou hast founded them.

(Ps. 89:11)

> The Lord is a great God,
>    and a great King above all gods.

> In his hand are the depths of the earth;
>   the heights of the mountains are his also.
> The sea is his, for he made it;
>   for his hands formed the dry land.

(Ps. 95:3–5)

> Know that the Lord is God!
>   It is he that made us, and we are his;
>   we are his people, and the sheep of his pasture.

(Ps. 100:3)

And *secondly* from the preaching of the great prophet of the Exile whom we call "Second Isaiah":

> But now thus says the Lord,
>   he who created you, O Jacob,
>   he who formed you, O Israel:
> Fear not, for I have redeemed you:
>   I have called you by name, you are mine.

(Isa. 43:1)

> Even to your old age I am He,
>   and to grey hairs I will carry you.
> I have made, and I will bear;
>   I will carry and will save.

(Isa. 46:4)

> Hearken to me, O Jacob,
>   and Israel, whom I called!
> I am he, I am the first,
>   and I am the last.
> My hand laid the foundation of the earth,
>   and my right hand spread out the heavens;
> when I call to them,
>   they stand forth together.

(Isa. 48:12–13)

In the first of these sets of passages we have expressed Israel's sense of gratitude as she praises God in the Temple. In the second it is Israel's sense of need that comes to the fore, as in exile in Babylon she waits for God to visit and redeem his people. The ground of her confidence in the one case and of her hope in the other is identical, God's sovereign will and power shown in Creation. He who made all things is Lord over all things and therefore Lord and Saviour of his people *now*.

(ii)

In the light of such references it is not only fitting, it was inevitable that the story of God's dealings with his people should begin with a declaration of faith in God as Creator. Israel had constantly to be reminded that the God who had, she thought, cast her adrift powerless in the midst of great and cruel nations was in charge of the world. Here in the chapter that opens her Scriptures she is given one of the most impressive of such reminders. As one by one his mighty acts in creating the world are rehearsed, she is being prepared for the later rehearsal of his mighty acts in her own election and redemption.

And her eyes are being lifted to a more distant future still, to a day when men and women everywhere would recognize her God as Lord and King. Had not God said when he promised to lead her forefather Abraham to a land that he would show him, "In you all the families of the earth will be blessed" (Gen. 12:3)? He intended nothing less than that all peoples should know and worship him. That was why he had chosen Israel. That indeed was why he had created the world. Having started the task with so overwhelming a display of his power, he could not, being God, do other than see it through to its conclusion.

(iii)

To take in all that is packed into the details of this great chapter cannot have been easy even for those for whom it was first composed, but they could at least grasp that message at its heart. We who study the chapter today have the added difficulty of finding its meaning for our own very different age, an age of science and technology which seems to have dismissed it as utterly outmoded. To close with the problems it raises will call for all our powers of concentration and thought.

All the more reason then for us to pause before we get embroiled in the business of probing and analysis and remind ourselves, as the ancient Hebrews had to be reminded, that its basic message for our age as for theirs is a very simple one. That is why to summarize it we could do worse than choose the words of a children's hymn, "He's got the whole world in his hands," especially when the last verse of the hymn brings it right down to each little child—"He's got you and me in his hands." A clever man wrote this chapter, and clever men have pondered it and argued about it ever since. But in the end of the day Creation yields its secret only to those who have the childlike faith to say

> God who made the earth,
>   The air, the sky, the sea,
> Who gave the light its birth,
>   Careth for me.

## GENESIS AND SCIENCE

Genesis 1:1–2:4(a) (*cont'd*)

One of the chief barriers that prevents Genesis Chapter 1 or for that matter Chapters 2 and 3 getting a fair hearing today is, as I have already hinted, the widely held opinion that they have been discredited by science.

(i)

It is often said that science is our guide and mentor now, not religion. Dr. Jacob Bronowski puts it like this: the fundamental assumption of our age "amounts to this, that science is to get rid of angels, blue fairies with red noses and other agents whose intervention would reduce the explanation of physical events to other than physical terms." By "other agents" he means, of course, a creating and governing God on the Genesis model. Science to him is essentially atheistic, and there is no doubt that many agree with him. Even pupils in our senior schools can ridicule Genesis' picture of how the world began and think they are saying something weighty and significant. "If you Christians believe that," we are told, "you will believe anything. How can anyone take seriously a God who fashioned the world in six days and who went for a walk in a garden called Eden and held conversations with snakes?"

We have all been faced with arguments like that, which set

science on a pedestal and quote the opening chapters of Genesis as a kind of stock example of the superstitions from which it has freed humankind.

### (ii)

The first thing to be said about such sneers is that they are probably much less prevalent nowadays than they used to be. It is sad to find a brilliant populariser of science like Dr. Bronowski indulging in them, but by and large it is not the scientists of today who claim that science has replaced God, but their more ignorant camp-followers who have as little idea of what science is really about as they have of religion. In fact a good number of our greatest scientists are sincere and practising Christians, and even those who are not are much less confident than were their predecessors of a generation ago that science has all the answers to the world's problems or is able to cure all the world's ills. We would be hard put to it to find many scientists, even atheistic scientists, who now argued that belief in God was necessarily incompatible with loyalty to scientific method.

At the same time Christians, too, have changed in their attitude to science. There must be very few who would today seriously contend that the world came into being in six days, or that man was constructed out of a lump of clay or woman from his spare rib. Most of us are willing to admit, and to admit freely, that the Church was wrong in the sixteenth century to anathematize Copernicus and Galileo for asserting that the earth moved round the sun, not the sun round the earth, and wrong in the nineteenth century to condemn Darwin for daring to suggest that human beings were descended from "monkeys". It was wrong because it tried to make out that Genesis was a textbook of science as well as being a textbook of faith.

### (iii)

In the twentieth century we are much more likely to claim for God the astounding universe which modern science has revealed, a universe of vast galaxies within which our earth and even our sun are but tiny specks, and a universe in which life has been slowly evolving over unimaginable millennia of time. That, not Genesis' little closed world of heaven up there and earth down here, is the universe that today's Christians believe God created. Far from diminishing him and making him an "unnecessary hypothesis", we would argue it immeasurably enhances his majesty—and his grace.

The Psalmist of old cried out in his amazement at it all:

> When I look at thy heavens, the work of thy fingers,
>   the moon and the stars which thou hast established;
> What is man that thou art mindful of him,
>   and the son of man that thou dost care for him?

(Ps. 8:3–4)

We in our turn are driven to awe and wonder, but it is before a universe which, thanks to science, we realize is infinitely more magnificent than anything the Psalmist could have conceived— yet its Creator is "mindful" of us!

We had a truly remarkable example of this change of attitude on the part of both scientists and Christians when in 1969 the American astronauts landed on the moon. For it was of all things to the first chapter of Genesis, to the very chapter that supercilious school children love to think has made the idea of God unfashionable, that they turned to express their feelings. Yet to the millions listening below on that historic occasion it did not sound at all peculiar to hear these well-known phrases coming back to earth from outer space—"In the beginning God created the heavens and the earth . . ." Quite the reverse, it seemed marvellously appropriate. There in the face of one of science's greatest achievements was an acknowledgment by the scientific community of a mystery at the heart of things which only religious words, not scientific ones, could adequately describe.

## GENESIS AND "MYTH"

Genesis 1:1–2:4(a) (*cont'd*)

The old bitter controversy between science and religion is, then, hopefully on the way to becoming a thing of the past. No one on either side takes up the extreme positions they once did.

But do we Christians really grasp the significance of this new attitude of ours towards science for our interpretation of Genesis? We are admitting that science is the proper source to turn to for factual knowledge about the physical origin and nature of the universe, and that Genesis' contribution to our understanding is a spiritual contribution. In effect we are treating this and the other opening chapters of Genesis as *imaginative stories,* approaching them as we would a modern short story or, to use a Biblical parallel, one of Our Lord's parables.

(i)

In doing so we are, if we only knew it, doing what the Hebrews themselves did. It is quite inconceivable that in an unlettered society like that of ancient Israel these chapters could have had their origin in some Hebrew equivalent of our universities or research institutes. They must have begun as folk tales. In ancient Israel ordinary people did not go to school or college but taught themselves and their children by the only means available to them, namely the stories they told to each other around the fireside at home or at their various social and religious gatherings. In other words they put into their stories not only what amused and entertained them but important matters of philosophy and culture as well.

As we now have the stories in Genesis, they have been revised, sometimes a little, sometimes a lot, by the scribes or "re-tellers" who gave them their written form and eventually made up a Bible out of them. But they are still stories. They would have got from the Hebrews who first heard them, as all good stories ought to get, a response of the imagination as well as of the intellect. It is a little sad that it has taken so many decades of painful and unnecessary strife between science and the Church for us to be willing to give them a similar response today. But at least we can be grateful that commonsense has at last prevailed.

(ii)

I am not so happy, however, about using the word *myth* to

describe the stories of Genesis. This is a word you will commonly find in academic books on Genesis. As the scholars
employ it, it indicates no more than a religious story about the
beginnings of things told by ancient peoples. It can thus be
applied equally to, for instance, the Hebrew story of the Flood
in Genesis Chapters 6 – 9 and to the Babylonian story of the
Flood in the eleventh tablet of the Gilgamesh epic cycle,
whatever difference there may be between these stories in
spiritual insight.

To the man-in-the-street, however, "myth" is a loaded word.
It almost invariably suggests an opinion or a belief that is
incredible or insincere or tendentious or even downright harmful. He may be willing to read the Flood story or any of the
other stories at the start of Genesis in an imaginative way, but if
he hears the word "myth" applied to them, he automatically
assumes not just that they come from an unsophisticated and
pre-scientific age but that they are unsophisticated and pre-
scientific nonsense. As long as there is a danger of this popular
rather than the academic sense being read into the word,
we are well advised to steer clear of it as much as we can.

The crucial insight I am trying to get across is not, then, that
Genesis is "myth"—a definition that raises more objections
than it removes—but that God in his wisdom chose to begin his
revelation of himself to mankind not in our own age when
people think "scientifically", but in an age three thousand years
and more ago when they thought about certain matters in the
form of imaginative stories. In order to understand what he is
saying to us about Creation today we have first to go back
across the centuries to that "simple" age and try to hear the
stories of Genesis as they would be heard by the Hebrews for
whom they were first intended. There is no short-cut if we wish
to do the job properly.

(iii)

I have spoken at some length about the opening chapters of
Genesis in relation to modern science and to what the scholars
call "myths", and I have spoken plainly. That is because I am

convinced that there is both on the side of believers and on the side of unbelievers a great deal of loose thinking which has to be cleared away before we can honestly and intelligently approach the task of interpreting these chapters for the present age. I hope that what I have said may be of help to many Christians who have got into the habit of avoiding them just because they raise in their minds an uncomfortable tension between their respect for the Bible and their respect for science. As I have tried to show, there need not be a clash.

I wish before going on, however, to add one footnote of the utmost importance. Nearly all the stories dealt with in this particular volume are imaginative stories in the sense I have talked about, and it would be easy for the reader to form the impression that I believed the whole Bible to be a "mythical" book. Nothing could be further from the truth. The great events by which God revealed himself to his people were *historical* events—in the Old Testament the call to Abraham, the deliverance from Egypt, the giving of the Law on Mount Sinai, the entry into the Promised Land, the emergence of the Davidic monarchy, the Exile in Babylon, and the return under Ezra to the Holy Land—and in the New Testament the birth and life and death and Resurrection of Our Lord, the inauguration of the New Covenant with God's new people, and the amazing spread of the infant Church into the Gentile world.

We know of these events because the people who witnessed and experienced them handed down reports of them, and it is these reports that make up the great bulk of the Bible from Genesis Chapter 12 onwards. Many of the reports are still cast in story form, and they can be rather thin on the kind of information that a professional historian likes to have. But that real history and not fiction lies behind these events there can be no possible doubt. We go to the Bible to have our own experience confirmed by the experience of God's people of old. We need have no fear that that experience with almost the sole exception of Genesis 1–11 (and a number of other passages dealing with the same subject of Creation) was based on things that actually happened.

I say "almost", for there is one other subject over and above Creation where "imagination" and not "fact" must be involved, namely what is to happen after death or at the end of the times. We should therefore be ready to recognize that a book like Revelation is also non-historical. In such matters as the beginning and end of the world, where by the very nature of the case no human testimony is possible, the writers of the Bible had to have the assistance of imagination and vision before they could say anything at all. But only there in the Bible does antiquity's habit of telling the stories the scholars call "myths" come into any prominence. Other ancient peoples did not have a direct personal encounter with the living God in the events of history, and for that reason their religions are "mythical" through and through. The religion of the Bible is at its core solidly and inescapably historical.

## ON TRANSLATING THE BIBLE'S FIRST TWO VERSES

Genesis 1:1–2

> In the beginning God created the heavens and the earth. The earth was without form and void, and darkness was upon the face of the deep; and the Spirit of God was moving over the face of the waters.

The two first verses of the Bible are so familiar that we rarely give them the attention they deserve. When we do begin to think about what they mean, we find that they are full of difficulties. We will have to spend a long time on them if we wish to do justice to their message for their own age and restate it authentically for our own.

(i)

Because of some unusual features in the Hebrew, they are difficult even to translate. Let us start by listing the three possible renderings:

(a)  We may follow the AV and the RSV (above) and take the

verses as separate sentences. This is the traditional rendering, being found in all the ancient versions (Greek, Latin, Syriac etc.).

(b) We may with the footnote in the RSV take verse 1 as introductory to verse 2, thus

> When God began to create the heavens and the earth, the earth was without form and void, and darkness was upon the face of the deep; and the Spirit of God was moving over the face of the waters.

This is the rendering favoured by most modern translations, e.g. Moffatt, NEB. Note, however, that for the last phrase Moffatt has

> ... *but* the spirit of God was hovering over the waters

while the NEB has after "void"

> ... with darkness over the face of the abyss, and a mighty wind [*lit.* wind of God] that swept over the surface of the waters.

The Hebrew word *ruach* means "wind" as well as "spirit", and the NEB follows not a few scholars in thinking it more suitable here.

(c) We may with several mediaeval Jewish commentators and some modern scholars take both verses 1 and 2 as introductory to verse 3, rendering along the following lines

> When God began to create the heavens and the earth, and when (as yet) the earth was without form and void, and there was darkness upon the face of the deep, and a mighty wind was blowing over the surface of the waters, then God said, "Let there be light."

Note that I have used here the NEB's "mighty wind" instead of "Spirit of God". This seems to me to be demanded by the different role now filled by verse 2. In (b) above there is a choice between making the last phrase of this verse a direct statement about what God was doing (RSV, Moffatt) and making it part of a description of what things were like at the time (NEB). But verse 2 is in this third arrangement wholly in parenthesis and only the second of these alternatives makes good sense. A direct statement about God at such a point would detract from the force of ". . . then God said" in verse 3, which on this rendering becomes the first positive statement of Scripture, to be followed immediately by God's own ringing words, "Let there be light!"

How are we to decide between these three translations, each of which is, on a linguistic level, equally acceptable? In the end my own preference is for (a), the traditional rendering, but I would emphasize *in the end*.

As I have just hinted, I am attracted by translation (c), because it brings into prominence God's thundering "Let there be light!" But that is not all. Its arrangement of the clauses very neatly parallels the beginning of the next story in Genesis, that of the Fall, in 2:4–7, which has a number of descriptive phrases ("In the day that . . . when . . . for . . . and . . . but . . .") leading up to an equally impressive climax—"then the Lord God formed man of dust from the ground . . . ."

Moreover, we find a similar arrangement at the opening of the Babylonian Creation story called (after its first two words) *Enuma Elish* or "When on high". I quote its first lines in full here not only to underline this point but because I shall be coming back to this story a number of times in the following pages. It goes:

When on high the heavens had not yet been named,
and below the firm ground had not yet been given a name,
when primaeval Apsu, their begetter,
and mother Tiamat, who gave them all birth,
still mingled their waters,
the reed had not yet sprung forth nor had the marsh appeared,
none of the gods had been brought into being,
they were still unnamed and their fortunes were not determined,
then the gods were created in their midst . . .
(translation by Hartmut Schmökel)

The climax here is the birth of the gods, a significantly different climax from "then God said, Let there be light!" or "then the Lord God formed man." But the parallel in language is impressive and suggests that the two stories in Genesis may have been composed in accordance with a widely accepted pattern in the ancient East.

There is, however, in spite of these parallels with Gen. 2 and the *Enuma Elish,* one important feature of translation (c) which leads me to reject it. My objection concerns the rendering "mighty wind" or literally "wind of God" which, as I argued, it almost demands. There does exist a Hebrew idiom which uses the phrase "of God" (*Elohim*) as a superlative, meaning "god-like" and therefore according to the context, "the highest, broadest, deepest, strongest possible etc." A good example is Ps. 36:6, where God is being addressed: "Thy righteousness is like the mountains of God," i.e. the loftiest mountains as contrasted with the lowest depths of the next line. Interestingly the older AV has here "great mountains", whereas the RSV has brought back "of God". Another example is Ps. 80:10 where it is the RSV which recognizes the idiom with "mighty cedars", while the AV retains "cedars of God".

But should we expect to find such an idiom in so carefully and indeed frugally worded a context as Gen. 1:1–3? Or for that matter in Gen. 1:1–2:4(a) as a whole, a document which contains no less than thirty-four other quite unambiguous occurrences of the word "God"? I think not. This chapter is no place for employing "God" in a figurative sense.

### (iii)

What then of translation (b)? Though he admits that many of his fellow scholars prefer it, Gerhard von Rad, I think, disposes of it in magisterial fashion when he observes that if one considers verses 1–2 as the syntactical unit, then the word about "chaos" would stand logically before the word about "creation". In other words, he is pointing out that the first positive statement in the Bible would be a statement not about God but about God's opposite. We will be examining later just what kind of a "chaos" verse 2 is describing. But for just now it is surely very difficult to argue with this powerful piece of theological insight.

We are driven back, therefore, on translation (a), which takes the two verses separately in the well-known traditional manner.

## IN THE BEGINNING GOD

Genesis 1:1–2 (*cont'd*)

There are still problems about how a separate verse 1 should be related to a separate verse 2, but let us postpone these for a little and turn our attention to drawing out further the meaning of verse 1 on its own.

(i)

Its opening words are *In the beginning God.* I have heard sermons preached on these four words which take the lesson to be that we must put God first in everything we do or think, because that is what the Bible does.

In my opinion such sermons completely miss the mark. They start from the typically modern assumption that we have a choice in the matter. When people today discuss theology, they automatically begin with the various arguments that can be advanced to prove (or if they are unbelievers, to disprove) the existence of God. We ourselves saw that this was so when we had to devote a whole section to the threat posed by scientific atheism to Biblical faith. But the Bible does not begin, "In the beginning there was a God." We have to take the whole sentence into account, not just four words. It begins "In the beginning God created . . . ." It takes God as given, almost, if you like, for granted, and focuses attention on his actions.

(ii)

The Hebrews would never have understood this habit of ours of treating God as a problem in philosophy. Nor, indeed, would any of the peoples in the ancient world of the Bible. Divinity, whether it was understood in terms of one God like the Hebrews, or of many gods like their neighbours, was simply there, as much a part of life as the air they breathed. Ancient peoples, the Hebrews included, could get themselves into a tangle of scepticism about what their God or gods were up to— we need only think of Ecclesiastes and his "All is vanity". Or they could, like Job, attack deity bitterly for what they thought was its unfairness and cruelty. But it was not open to either Job or Ecclesiastes—as it is unfortunately all too open to us—to doubt that deity existed. The peoples of antiquity did not want to have the choice of deciding to put God first which we think we can make, and they would not know what we were talking about if we offered it to them.

Far from being an invitation to us to give God the first place in our lives and feel good for doing it, the first verse of the Bible is a searing *rebuke* from a God-filled past to a godless present, from an ancient world that could not think at all without the idea of God to a modern world that regards the idea of God as an optional extra. That is what sermons on this great verse should be saying.

## THE TRANSCENDENCE OF GOD

Genesis 1:1–2 (*cont'd*)

*In the beginning God created.* God is our Creator and therefore our Lord. That, as we saw, is the simplest lesson to be taken from this chapter and therefore from its opening verse which first states its leading thought, the lesson of the sovereignty of God. It is more difficult for us to see a second lesson implied in the phrase *God created,* that of God's transcendence.

(i)

We are thinking now not of the Creator as he acts towards us but as he is in himself, and that is something that we cannot really put into words. Human words like human thought belong this side of Creation and cannot begin to describe its other side, God as he is in his own interior life.

Nevertheless, we have to try. We can start by admitting that if we are *absolutely* dependent on God as sovereign Lord of the world, then by definition he is *absolutely* independent of us. We need him, but he does not need us. In himself God is "before" time and "beyond" space, and only enters time and space because he wants to. In himself he is "outside" nature and is only to be found "inside" it in the relative sense that a painting contains some information about the artist who painted it. Even the knowledge of him that we gain from his special revelation of himself in the history of Israel and the life of Jesus Christ has to be owned to be a relative knowledge. In himself God is the Wholly Other, unconditioned except as he decides to impose conditions on himself, self-sufficient except as he decides to bring others into being on whom he can lavish the love which he has to spare.

All this and more is what is involved when we speak of the *transcendence* of God, and it is summed up better by the concept of Creation than in any other way. God is the Creator, and we and all other existing animals and things are his creatures.

(ii)

It cannot be too often emphasized that this idea of God's transcendence over the natural order is a uniquely Biblical idea. It conflicts not only with the thinking of the age in which the Bible was written but with the thinking of the modern age to which we belong.

The typical ancient conception of Creation is in fact hardly "creation" in a real sense at all. We can see this from the opening lines of the *Enuma Elish* quoted some pages ago. It speaks of two deities, a male Apsu and a female Tiamat, mingling their waters. These waters are the same as the "waters" of Gen. 1:2 and 1:6–7, which the Hebrews' God separated into two by constructing the vault of heaven. In other words, Apsu and Tiamat are personifications of a primaeval watery "chaos", and it is they who "beget" and "give birth to" the other gods. One of these gods called Marduk eventually defeats "chaos" by killing Tiamat, and makes the heavens and the earth out of her corpse and human beings out of the blood of one of her henchmen. As a reward for his victory over Tiamat, Marduk is given the kingship over the other gods and over the universe.

It comes as no surprise to us to learn that Marduk was the chief deity of the Babylonians among whom this particular "myth" took its rise. The story in essence reflects the way in which the Babylonians regarded the hostile and friendly forces in nature and in politics, all of which are either themselves deities or under the tutelage of a particular deity, with their own favourite god Marduk being the most powerful and the kindest among them. Nothing in it takes us outside the known world. It sometimes uses the language of begetting and bearing offspring and sometimes the language of fashioning and making, but in the last analysis all the Babylonian gods are *immanent,* themselves part of the natural order they are supposed to control. There is no transcendence.

(iii)

And what of modern thinking (modern thinking, that is, which is sympathetic to the idea of God)? For an example of a representative and influential modern understanding of the relation between God and the world of nature I suggest we turn to William Wordsworth and the Lakeland poets. I choose them rather than a philosophic treatment of the subject because as poets they are not only likely to be more familiar to ordinary folks but likely to have made a more profound and lasting impression on their minds and hearts.

You will know the kind of approach to nature that I mean, the kind of approach that speaks of nature as the language in which God expresses his thoughts or as the mirror which reflects his image, that speaks of the Divine wisdom within nature carrying the soul back to itself in her reflected beams, or of the footprints of Divine beauty which may be traced everywhere in the countryside around us. It is an approach that is movingly commended in Wordsworth's *Lines Composed above Tintern Abbey,* when he describes

> . . . that serene and blessed mood,
> In which the affections gently lead us on,—
> Until, the breath of this corporeal frame
> And even the motion of our human blood
> Almost suspended, we are laid asleep
> In body, and become a living soul:
> While with an eye made quiet by the power
> Of harmony, and the deep power of joy,
> We see into the life of things.

Or when later in the same poem he feels himself to be in touch with

> A presence that disturbs one with the joy
> Of elevated thoughts; a sense sublime
> Of something far more deeply interfused,
> Whose dwelling is the light of setting suns,
> And the round ocean and the living air,
> And the blue sky, and in the mind of man:
> A motion and a spirit, that impels
> All thinking things, all objects of all thought,
> And rolls through all things.

On the surface such an attitude to the world of nature often seems not incompatible with the Biblical attitude. But is it not in fact simply the *Enuma Elish* brought up to date? Does it not identify God with his creation, so that in communing (a favourite word of people who think like Wordsworth) with nature we are in effect communing with God?

It may be going too far to describe it as pantheism, the doctrine that God is everything and everything is God, which is a very intellectual notion. But it is certainly a sort of emotional nature-mysticism, a seeking after an absorption in the "All", which can, depending on one's preference at the time, be called either God or nature. It has little real connection with the Biblical idea of transcendence, which resolutely distances the Creator from his creation. On an emotional level (which is, of course, an extremely important one when reading poetry) nature-poets like Wordsworth are seductive and can indeed be uplifting. But a bit of hard thinking should lead us to be wary of them in matters of theology.

## NEW EVERY MORNING

Genesis 1:1–2 (*cont'd*)

(iv)

Let us now go on to examine the way the Old Testament itself pictures a transcendent Creator, and we will see more clearly just how unique the Biblical view is compared with the non-Biblical views we have been looking at.

This means above all appreciating the devastating evidence of the verb "create" itself, in Hebrew as in the related language of Phoenicia *bara*. Other similar Hebrew verbs like "make" (*ʿasah*) and "form" (*yatsar*) can have either God or a human being as subject. Phoenician can apply the participle of *bara, boré* ("creator"), to a craftsman in metal. In English we can speak of the "creativity" of the artist. But in Hebrew the subject of *bara* is invariably and solely God. When as in the present verse it refers to his work in the original Creation there is never any mention of the material used. But just as often the verb refers to God's present and future activity. In these references it is tantamount to "transform". The nuances are of the new, the unexpected, the perturbing, the miraculous. And all through there is a constant stress on God's incomparability.

The following are among the most illuminating examples:

(of Israel's future)

> Behold, I make a covenant. Before all your people I will do marvels, such as have not been wrought [lit. *created*] in all the earth or in any nation; and all the people among whom you are shall see the work of the Lord; for it is a terrible thing that I will do with you.
>
> (Exod. 34:10)

(of the fate of the Korahites)

But if the Lord *creates* something new, and the ground opens its mouth, and swallows them up, with all that belongs to them, and they go down alive into Sheol, then you shall know that these men have despised the Lord.

(Num. 16:30)

(of the transformation of the sinner)

*Create* in me a clean heart, O God,
  and put a new and right spirit within me.

(Ps. 51:10)

(of God's incomparability)

For who in the skies can be compared to the Lord?
  Who among the heavenly beings is like the Lord?
......
The north and the south, thou hast *created* them;
  Tabor and Hermon joyously praise thy name.

(Ps. 89:6,12)

(again)

To whom then will you compare me,
  that I should be like him?
  says the Holy One.
Lift up your eyes on high and see:
  who *created* these?

(Isa. 40:25–26)

(again)

Thus says God, the Lord,
  who *created* the heavens and stretched them out
......
"I am the Lord, that is my name;
  my glory I give to no other,
  nor my praise to graven images.
Behold, the former things have come to pass,
  and new things I now declare;
before they spring forth
  I tell you of them."

(Isa. 42:5,8–9)

(of the joy to come in the latter days)

> For behold, I *create* new heavens and a new earth;
> and the former things shall not be remembered
>    or come into mind.
> But be glad and rejoice for ever
>    in that which I *create*;
> for behold, I *create* Jerusalem a rejoicing,
>    and her people a joy.

(Isa. 65:17–18)

(and finally, for a change, an ironical use)

> For the Lord has *created* a new thing on the earth:
>    a woman protects a man!

(Jer. 31:22)

(v)

There can be no doubt that the usage of the Hebrew verb "create" powerfully underscores the transcendence of the One who creates. He alone can be its subject. No material is mentioned. He cannot be compared with any other god or with anything in his creation. Nor can he be tied down or forestalled. He created and he still creates, and therefore his world is full of surprises, pleasant and not so pleasant, and the life of humanity is fraught with the possibility of new beginnings. As the poet of Lamentations puts it in a sudden flash of hope amid his bitter complaints: "His mercies never come to an end; they are new every morning" (Lam. 3:22–23).

## THE PROBLEM OF GENESIS CHAPTER ONE VERSE TWO

Genesis 1:1–2 (*cont'd*)

Most of us move quickly from verse 1 to verse 3, and either do not hear or silently ignore the discordant note sounded by the verse in between. We are wrong to do so. There is a problem in verse 2, a serious problem, which needs to be properly appreciated. Once it is, the verse is seen to add a very necessary layer of realism to the Biblical teaching on Creation, without which the hopeful notes that teaching sounds could be regarded as little more than wishful thinking.

(i)

We have just been contrasting the way in which Israel and her neighbours thought about the origin of the world. In the *Enuma Elish* the gods are from the start part of nature, and in the story of their marriages and squabbles we see reflected the Babylonians' belief in the emergence of an ordered cosmos out of a primaeval chaos. Very different is the Hebrew conception of a single transcendent God who *really* creates, that is, who gives to everything its existence and is not to be confused with what he makes. To us this is the meaning of verse 1, and we cannot see how it differs greatly from the orthodox Jewish and Christian doctrine of *creatio ex nihilo* or "creation out of nothing". We automatically expect the chapter to go on to describe a series of God's actions which we can interpret in terms of that doctrine. And the chapter appears to oblige. In verse 3 we have the splendid "God spoke . . . and it was done!" of the creation of light on the first day, and there are similar phrases to introduce what happened on the other five days.

It is therefore not a little disconcerting to find that if we read verse 2 and some of the following verses more closely, they seem just like the Babylonian account to be tracing the beginning of the world back to a kind of chaos. We have to wait till verses 9 and 10 before we can speak safely of anything that resembles a completed cosmos. Only then does the earth described in verse 2 as "without form and void" become the dry land, and the dark deep of the same verse become what we now call the seas. And only then do we have God's verdict that they are good.

Does this mean that God created the chaos, or, worse, that it was there in the beginning, independent of him? The chapter does not give an unequivocal answer.

(ii)

The old Rabbis and the Fathers of the Church used to get out of this logical impasse by taking verse 1 to refer to an original and perfect Creation "out of nothing", which then "fell" or collapsed Lucifer-like into the chaos pictured in verse 2. After this God had, as it were, to begin again, so that our chapter is in effect describing a second Creation in which God has to take account of chaos. I don't think anyone is going to be persuaded by such a theory nowadays. It is entirely speculative, assuming not only a first Creation but also a first Fall, of neither of which is there any hint elsewhere in Scripture.

### (iii)

Today's scholars are much more likely to explain the problem as due to a failure of language. They see in verse 2 a survival from an earlier and more robust Hebrew story of Creation, which was more affected by the "myths" of Israel's environment and which the author of this chapter was not quite able to "rewrite" completely. We find further echoes of this older story in poetic passages like Ps. 74:12–14 or Isa. 51:9, where there are allusions to God defeating a monster of chaos called Leviathan or Rahab, who must have been a popular Hebrew counterpart of the Babylonian Tiamat. Daring as ever, the poets were not, it seems, troubled by the colourful personifications of the popular tradition. But according to these scholars the more careful author of Genesis Chapter 1 has made a sustained effort to rid this tradition of its noise and conflict and has left in place of its violent chaos little more than empty space and dark silent waters. Over this lifeless scene only the Spirit of God is stirring, poised to transform it into the world we know.

There is thus, they would claim, no essential clash with the doctrine of *creatio ex nihilo*. Verse 1 has taken care of that, for it has just stated that God created the whole universe, and that must include the inert and harmless stuff on which he now sets to work. They would prefer that the author had got rid altogether of such vestiges of chaos, but seen in perspective they are mere pinpricks and need not worry us too much.

This modern interpretation is an attractive one, but I am not convinced that it will do.

## THE DIMENSION OF EVIL

Genesis 1:1–2 (*cont'd*)

### (iv)

As I react to it, there is in Gen. 1:2 much more than a lingering whiff of the battle between God and the monster.

Let me quote in full the poetic passages to which we have just referred. First the Psalm (74):

Yet God my King is from of old,
  working salvation in the midst of the earth.
Thou didst divide the sea by thy might;
  thou didst break the heads of the dragons on the waters.
Thou didst crush the heads of Leviathan,
  thou didst give him as food for the creatures of the wilderness.

Then the prophet (Isa. 51):

Awake, awake, put on strength,
  O arm of the Lord;
awake, as in days of old,
  the generations of long ago.
Was it not thou that didst cut Rahab in pieces,
  that didst pierce the dragon?

Now let me add a passage which brings in not a chaos dragon but the chaos waters of our verse:

The floods have lifted up, O Lord,
  the floods have lifted up their voice,
  the floods lift up their roaring.
Mightier than the thunders of many waters,
  mightier than the waves of the sea,
  the Lord on high is mighty.

(Ps. 93:3–4)

And finally, one in which the battle with the dragon takes place in the future:

In that day the Lord with his hard and great and strong sword will punish Leviathan the fleeing serpent, Leviathan the twisting serpent, and he will slay the dragon that is in the sea.

(Isa. 27:1)

(v)

We surely cannot be dealing here simply with a remnant of an older and cruder Hebrew story of Creation. The monster and the waters are not simply figures of a chaos that once was, but also of one that God has to defeat now and that he will have to defeat in the last days.

In other words, they are figures of a real power of evil in God's world, a power that once tried to thwart his will and for all that he repulsed it then, tries to do so still. They are nothing less than the Old Testament's equivalent of the Devil and the "principalities and powers" of the New Testament. I admit that the studied prose of this chapter steers clear of the hyperbole of the poets. But the language it uses comes from the same background and I cannot believe that it wants to remove all of its menace and imaginative nuance. There is a lot more to verse 2 than a description of inert primal material.

There can be no doubt that the Hebrews dreaded chaos as a reality, present in the beginning, present now, and potentially present in the future. It was especially associated in their minds with the waters now kept at bay outside the firmament and beneath the earth, but once enveloping everything. At any moment these waters could return, so that whenever a storm arose there was always the fear that their universe was about to collapse. But by the way their poets constantly and luridly harped upon them, it is evident that they feared more than the waters themselves. It is this very real chaos, a physical thing but also a spiritual thing, that our verse in its quieter way is conjuring up before us.

(vi)

We no longer in this modern age accept the view which the ancient Hebrews held of the physical world with its flat earth and its dome-like sky and, as we have now found out, its great deep beyond. We have long since replaced their understanding with our scientific understanding. But as we transfer God as Creator from their universe to our universe, we would be very ill-advised not to listen to the sinister overtones of this verse.

At bottom the problem of Gen. 1:2 is not the obvious one of our modern distaste at ancient ways of putting things but the problem of the origin of evil, that age-old conundrum of theology which no one has yet satisfactorily solved.

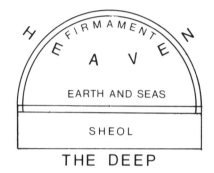

As it happens, the Old Testament as a whole is much more inclined than we are to attribute evil to God's direct will. The author of this chapter does not say in so many words that he created chaos, but that is the implication of verse 1, and I am sure that if pressed he would admit it, though he would not understand our discomfort. See, for instance, Isa. 45:6–7 (a chapter that has not a few points of contact with Gen. 1 and to which we shall be returning shortly):

> I am the Lord, and there is no other.
> I form light and create darkness,
> I make weal and create woe.

Or if we are thinking of the monster, Job 40:15, 19 (where it is given yet another name):

> Behold, Behemoth,
> which I made as I made you
> . . . . . .
> He is the first of the works of God.

But let us not get too bogged down in our theological logic. Our chapter is above all a positive account of God's creation of the world stressing its order and its goodness and setting forth his sovereignty and transcendence. It is not by chance that verse 1 comes before verse 2. Nevertheless, the Hebrews were realistic enough to realize that behind the order and the light and the goodness lurked disorder and darkness and evil. So verse 2 forcibly, but for the moment fleetingly, recalls this power of evil to our minds before the chapter in verse 3 returns to its main theme.

## CHAOS . . . . . .

Genesis 1:1–2 (*cont'd*)

We are now ready to go through the component parts of verse 2 and see how far we can reconstruct in detail the picture it presented to the people who first heard it. This will enable us to spell out further the very realistic and therefore genuinely comforting lesson which I believe it has to teach us.

(i)

*First,* there is the earth "without form and void". It is my opinion that much of our trouble in understanding verse 2 stems from this particular rendering, which is not demanded by the Hebrew. I suspect it owes more to later Greek ideas than most scholars have allowed. Certainly it is not greatly different from the translations found in two of the ancient Greek versions, the "invisible and unformed" of the Septuagint and the "emptiness and nothing" of Aquila's version.

The Greeks generally thought of chaos as empty space, a kind of insubstantial stuff as opposed to the cosmos of the organized material world, and in their more philosophical moments they could even speak of it as "not being" over against the "being" of the cosmos. It is not a large step from these rather refined notions to the orthodox Judeo-Christian doctrine of *creatio ex nihilo,* so there would be considerable pressure on the Greek-

speaking Jews who were responsible for the Septuagint and its
sister versions to move their renderings in the direction they
did. Like all good translators they were trying to make the Bible
meaningful to their contemporaries. But I feel that they may
have gone too far in this case and all but lost touch with the
original Hebrew.

The Hebrew phrase is *tohu wa-bohu,* two nouns (not adjec-
tives) joined by "and". The second noun *bohu* is not found
elsewhere on its own, but *tohu* occurs a number of times. It has
the physical meaning "desert" or "wasteland" (e.g. Job 6:18),
but it is used also in various figurative senses to refer, e.g., to the
"vanity" of idols (1 Sam. 12:21), to the "worthlessness" of the
nations in God's eyes (Isa. 40:17), to the "falsity" of pleas in
court (Isa. 59:4). One could argue that these senses are linked
together by the central idea of "emptiness", but I think it is more
likely that all of them go back to a proper association of the
word with the Creation story. Whatever was considered to be
like chaos was called in Hebrew *tohu.*

This is certainly true of the two occasions on which the full
phrase occurs other than in the present verse. The passages are
Isa. 34:11 and Jer. 4:23, both poetic descriptions of God's
coming judgment which paint it in vision as in effect chaos-
come-again. The contexts speak of streams being turned into
pitch, of the land becoming waste and devastated, of the
heavens darkening and the mountains quaking, of the flight of
men and birds from the scene. Nearly all of the images are
violent ones and make us think of the desolation or confusion
left behind by an earthquake or a whirlwind or an invading
army rather than of mere emptiness. The passages were composed by poets, but due allowance being made for that, it seems
to me reasonable to assume that they were more on the wave-
length of the author of this chapter than Jewish emigrants
translating it into Greek many centuries later.

I would therefore fill out the picture as in the following
translation:"(Where) the earth (was later to be, there) was
chaos and confusion"—or perhaps better: "(What was later to
be called) the earth was (as yet) desolation and disorder." The

two alliterative pairs of nouns are my attempts to catch in English the weird flavour of the Hebrew *tohu wa-bohu.*

### (ii)

*Secondly,* there are the dark waters of the great deep. With these we come to an element of chaos in Hebrew thinking that is not found in Greek thinking. We would be well advised therefore not to substitute "abyss" for "deep" as several modern translations do (e.g. Moffatt, NEB). The word "abyss" is of Greek origin and suggests bottomlessness, but it has no necessary connection with waters.

The Hebrew word for "the deep" is *tehom,* which as verse 7 makes clear was thought of as consisting of two halves which had originally been one, namely the waters under the firmament and the waters above it. These waters came down through the firmament as rain by means of "windows" (Gen. 7:11) or "sluices" (Job 38: 25; the RSV has "channel"), and up through the earth as springs and rivers and seas. In most of its Old Testament occurrences *tehom* denotes our actual sea or ocean (Job 28:14; 38:16). But it is not restricted to the sea. In Deut. 8:7 it is used in the plural as a name for the "springs" which came from the same source, and in Ezek. 31:4 it is described as feeding the Nile and the other rivers of Egypt.

Finally there are a couple of passages in the Psalms (77:16; 104:5–9) where it has the same reference to the events of Creation as here. These are for our purpose the most interesting of all. We are again dealing with poetic passages, which are full of picturesque and indeed rather extravagant expressions. But again I would argue that we should not put too wide a gap between what was allowable in poetry and what was thought appropriate by the prose author of Genesis Chapter 1.

Psalm 77:16 reads:

> When the waters saw thee, O God,
>> when the waters saw thee, they were afraid,
>> yea, the deep trembled.

Ps. 104 speaks of the deep covering the earth as a garment and the waters standing above the mountains, and then goes on (verse 7):

> At thy rebuke they fled;
>> at the sound of thy thunder they took to flight.
> The mountains rose, the valleys sank down
>> to the place which thou didst appoint for them.
> Thou didst set a bound which they should not pass,
>> so that they might not again cover the earth.

The language of trembling, fleeing, being contained, which we meet in these passages is much more robust than the relatively colourless verbs "separate" and "gather together" of verses 4, 6–7 and 9–10 in Gen. 1, but we cannot deny that the theme is the same.

We have probably then to think in verse 2 of a confused and desolate "something", which was later to become the earth, but which is at this moment still immersed in or surrounded by the swirling waters of an all-encompassing deep. That to the Hebrews was the chaos with which Creation began. It is far removed from the calm and motionless scene which under the influence of English translations like "without form and void" or "abyss" we usually, but quite misleadingly, envisage. On the contrary, it is distinctly menacing and frightening, and it almost invites the spiritual interpretation as the power of evil which we have argued is attached to it both in this verse and in the Psalms and prophetic oracles with which we have compared it.

## . . . . . . CONFRONTED BY GOD

Genesis 1:1–2 (*cont'd*)

We have anticipated it in nearly every passage we have quoted, but now at last we have it in Genesis' own words—God's answer to chaos. *But*—not *and*—*the Spirit of God was moving over the face of the waters.* High above chaos God himself was active, about to send·down life and light into the midst of death's darkness and to challenge its power with a greater power.

(i)

Once more the Hebrew words denote movement and energy, even violence, and once more we have to counter English translations which miss the point. A favourite one is of the Spirit "brooding" over the waters. This gives a touching picture of God's concern if the comparison is with the mother bird sitting on her eggs, but a more virile one if the comparison is with the father bird, as in Milton's *Paradise Lost:*

> ... thou from the first
> Wast present, and with mighty wings outspread
> Dove-like sat'st brooding on the vast abyss,
> And mad'st it pregnant.

Milton is merely developing the figure of speech as he finds it in Genesis with help from Matt. 3:16 or John 1:32. But more recently, those who scour ancient mythologies have told us that ideas of a world-egg are not uncommon in them, the world being thought of as hatched from a fluid chaos. A few modern Biblical scholars have picked up these references and suggested that a primitive notion of that kind may lie behind the phrase here. But quite apart from its crudity, there is no evidence that such a notion was current in Israel's immediate environment. And even if it were, the author of this chapter would be hardly likely to bring it in alongside a description of chaos that has so far been consistently of a watery confusion needing to be contained.

The Hebrew verb translated "was moving" in the RSV (it is similarly rendered in the ancient versions) occurs only once elsewhere in the Old Testament, in the old poem preserved in Deut. 32, which speaks of God's care for Israel. Verses 10 to 12 read:

> He found him in a desert land,
>   and in the howling *waste* of the wilderness;
> he encircled him, he cared for him,
>   he kept him as the apple of his eye.
> Like an eagle that stirs up its nest,
>   that *flutters over* its young,

spreading out its wings, catching them,
    bearing them on its pinions,
the Lord alone did lead him,
    and there was no foreign god with him.

Note that I have italicized not only "flutters over", which is how
the RSV renders the verb here, but "waste", which is none other
in Hebrew than *tohu*. It seems that we have yet another poetic
passage making use of the Creation story, and yet again the
context is a violent one. The poet is picturing God finding his
people in the wilderness and protecting them from their
enemies as an eagle guards its nest against intruders, flying
around flapping its wings then plunging down to carry its
fledglings off to a safe place.

No doubt the use of the same verb describing a bird in
Deuteronomy encouraged the speculations about "brooding"
in Gen. 1:2. But the bird is an eagle, not Milton's dove, and
there is a long way to go from "fluttering" to "brooding".
Moffatt's "hovering" is a kind of half-way house and was
perhaps chosen in order that options might be left open.
However, Moffatt has *but* at the start of the phrase, and so is
contrasting chaos and God. I also prefer *but* to *and,* but I would
go a lot further than either "was moving" or "was hovering".

The chaos is not in this verse, as Israel is in the poem in
Deuteronomy, the object of God's protecting concern but
rather the enemy to be driven off. I suggest something like
"soaring" or "wheeling" or "swooping". The NEB is on the right
lines with its wind "that swept" over the waters (though you will
recall that we could not follow its interpretation of the phrase).

(ii)

God's Spirit then is compared to an eagle swooping down to
ward off its enemies. This may seem to us an unsuitable
metaphor, but that is probably because like Milton we have in
our minds the descent of the Spirit on Our Lord at his baptism
by John. But in fact that is the only place in the Bible where that
particular comparison is made. It is a beautiful image, taken up
in many of our hymns, as in John Keble's

> Softer than gale at morning prime,
> Hovered his holy Dove

—though it will be noticed how Keble preserves himself from sentimentality with the intentionally dissonant "gale". He is well aware of the word's other meaning, and indeed goes on in his hymn to celebrate Pentecost's "rushing mighty wind". Even in the New Testament then it is God's presence *in power* that the Spirit chiefly represents.

How much more true is this of the Old Testament! The Spirit of God or of the Lord is the power from which no one can escape (Ps. 139:7). It is the power that fits Israel's judges to lead her in war (Judg. 6:34; 14:6). It is the power that equips the prophets to preach (Num. 11:25; Isa. 61:1). It is the power that lies behind the extraordinary ability of some individuals (Gen. 41:38; Exod. 31:3). And it is the power that gives life to *all* living creatures, without which they must perish (Job 33:4; Ps. 104:29).

It is undoubtedly the last of these, the Spirit as life-giver, that is the main thought in our verse. The picture is not, however, as I hope I have to say for the last time, of God supplying life to a corpse-like material, but of God opposing the principle of life to the principle of death which was embodied in the desolation and darkness of the *tohu* and the *tehom*.

## A GOSPEL IN EMBRYO

Genesis 1:1–2 (*cont'd*)

We may at this point usefully sum up where we have reached so far.

### (i)

The first two verses of Genesis are like the counterweights on a pair of scales. Both are needed to achieve the correct balance of faith. With a marvellous sureness of touch they place together God and chaos, good and evil, so that we do not question the reality of either, yet are at the same time convinced that only one will ultimately triumph.

They say to us: "Don't forget the Evil One, but first and foremost and all the time put your trust in God, who created all things and is therefore Lord of all things." Far from speaking only of what happened in the remote past, they direct our attention to what God is doing now and what he has still to do before the purpose for which he created the world is finally realized. Like every doctrine of the faith, the doctrine of Creation is in the final analysis a Gospel in embryo.

(ii)

Again I turn to the great poet of the Exile to find the words to clothe the bare bones of Genesis Chapter 1 with flesh. I have already quoted Isa. 45:7 ("I form light and create darkness") as an example of Israel's forthright ideas about the origin of evil, ideas which the author of this story must have shared though he is more circumspect than the poet about the way he phrases them. Later in the same chapter we meet another passage that reminds us of the Creation story, as the prophet warns the exiles not to have anything to do with idols. Verses 18 and 19 go on:

> For thus says the Lord,
>   who created the heavens
>   (he is God!),
> who formed the earth and made it
>   (he established it;
> he did not create it a chaos [*tohu*],
>   he formed it to be inhabited!):
> "I am the Lord, and there is no other.
> I did not speak in secret,
>   in a land of darkness;
> I did not say to the offspring of Jacob,
>   'Seek me in chaos.'
> I the Lord speak the truth,
>   I declare what is right."

The prophet is clearly comparing the gods of the nations with the chaos that preceded Creation. They are like the desolate earth of verse 2 here, menacing but in the last resort powerless either to hurt or to save. For God did not create the earth to remain a chaos, but to be inhabited, to be a place where he could meet and speak with his people in truth.

Indeed, the end for which he created the world was even as they despaired coming to pass before their eyes, when (verse 22) he could issue his great invitation:

> Turn to me and be saved,
>   all the ends of the earth!
>   For I am God, and there is no other.
> By myself I have sworn,
>   from my mouth has gone forth in righteousness
>   a word that shall not return:
> "To me every knee shall bow,
>   every tongue shall confess."

## THE FIRST OF DAYS—AND GOD SAID

Genesis 1:3–5

And God said, "Let there be light"; and there was light. And God saw that the light was good; and God separated the light from the darkness. God called the light Day, and the darkness he called Night.

And there was evening and there was morning, one day.

We have chaos and we have God's presence in his Spirit. The scene is set for the story of Creation to unwind. It is, as our chapter presents it, a movement away from chaos towards cosmos, from disorder towards order, from desolation towards fruitfulness. The movement lasts six days, and the first of these opens with an explosion of light amid the primaeval darkness. Or does it? Rather it begins with the sound of God's voice speaking.

(i)

*And God said.* This simple phrase occurs so many hundred times in the Bible that we can never hope to exhaust its significance. In this context of Creation we can perhaps best pinpoint what the author has in mind by recalling our earlier discussions of verse 1 and of the Hebrew verb *bara* which carries so much of the weight of its meaning.

He is thinking, therefore, of God's sovereignty—he speaks and things exist.

> **By the word of the Lord the heavens were made**
> . . . . . .
> For he spoke, and it came to be;
> he commanded, and it stood forth.
>
> (Ps. 33:6,9)

He is thinking of God's transcendence—he speaks and only then *can* things exist, for only a transcendent God can really create.

> **Who has directed the Spirit of the Lord,**
> or as his counsellor has instructed him?
>
> (Isa. 40:13)

He is thinking of God's purposive will—he speaks this time, and he speaks seven times more (verses 6, 9, 11, 14, 20, 24, 26), and a whole ordered universe exists.

> . . . . . .
> so shall my word be that goes forth from my mouth;
> it shall not return to me empty,
> but it shall accomplish that which I purpose,
> and prosper in the thing for which I sent it.
>
> (Isa. 55:11)

And he is thinking of God's grace—he speaks and *we* exist. If he begins Creation by speaking, he must be seeking others to speak with him—and that means us human beings. Simply by speaking, then, God reveals what it is ultimately all about. He has done with solitude and is embarking on an adventure of love which can only end when all men and women everywhere freely love him in return.

### (ii)

God said . . . *and there was* . . . , or as we usually have it elsewhere in the chapter, *And it was so* (verses 6–7, 9, 11, 14–15, 24, 29–30).

Probably without thinking we assume this to mean that as soon as God uttered his word of command, the light, the firmament, the sun and moon and the rest came into being just like that. A careful look at Gen. 1 shows that this is not the case.

It may only say in verse 3 that God called the light into existence, but both in verse 7 and in verse 16 it is specifically stated that God also "made" the firmament and the heavenly bodies. Similarly in verse 21 God "created" the fish and the birds, in verse 25 he "made" the animals, and in verse 27 he "created" man. It is the same in Psalm 33, where just after "By the word of the Lord the heavens were made" and just before "he spoke, and it came to be", the poet talks of him "gathering" the waters of the sea in a bottle and "putting" the deeps in storehouses (verse 7). Obviously creation by the word of God did not to the Hebrew mind exclude the idea of God himself doing the work, but was simply an alternative way of expressing the same thought.

To get at the author's intention in using this phrase we have to remember that to everyone in the age of the Bible the uttered word—anybody's word—was a very mysterious and powerful thing. It was invested almost with a life of its own, and was believed, once spoken, to begin immediately to act. That is one of the reasons why in the Bible the book of Proverbs is so full of warnings against rash talk.

> When words are many, transgression is not lacking,
> but he who restrains his lips is prudent.
>
> (Prov. 10:19)

It explains, too, why even though he wanted to, Isaac was unable to revoke the blessing which he had pronounced on Jacob, thinking him to be his elder brother Esau—he had to say "yes, and he shall be blessed" (Gen. 27:33).

The author of Gen. 1, then, was doing no more than searching for a form of words that would do justice to the effectiveness of a command *of God.* His solution, almost naive

in its simplicity, is "And it was so." He is not with this phrase
making a philosophical point as our traditional doctrine of
"creation out of nothing" does, namely that before God spoke
there was "nothing" and after it "something"—that may be
implied, but is of more interest to us than it was to him. Nor is
he emphasizing the suddenness or speed with which things
happened—God had still to do the making. He is drawing our
attention to the fact that in this case it was the sovereign Lord of
Creation who spoke—and who then went on to make. There is
no more to it than that.

(iii)

No more to it than that? Yet how much that is!

Martin Buber records a story about Rabbi Sussya of Hanipol
which goes right to the heart of what I have been trying to say in
this section. It goes right to the heart of it by suggesting in its
typically Jewish way that I shouldn't have been saying anything
at all! Whenever his master, the great Maggid, was reading a
passage of Scripture which he wished to expound and uttered
the words "And God said" or "And God spoke", Rabbi Sussya
used to become so agitated that he had to be led from the room.
And there in the corridor outside he would hammer with his
fists on the wall and cry out in ecstasy, "And God spoke!",
"And God spoke!" He did not calm down until the Maggid had
finished his sermon. So it was said of him that he never heard
his master's teaching, yet knew more of what he taught than his
most attentive disciple.

There is a Christian story which also reminds us that wonder
not explanation is the only proper reaction to God's living and
creating word. It is the well-known story of God's Son calming
the storm on the Sea of Galilee. It ends with a single abrupt
sentence which like Rabbi Sussya's peculiar antics carries us
back in our minds to the first Creation:

> And they were filled with awe, and said to one another, "Who then is
> this, that even wind and sea obey him?"

(Mark 4:41)

## THE FIRST OF DAYS—LET THERE BE LIGHT!

Genesis 1:3–5 (*cont'd*)

(iv)

God said *Let there be light!* And there was light.

This is a very dramatic phrase, deeply embedded in the imaginations of both Jew and Christian. And it was of course intended to appeal to the imagination. But it is also worth remembering that it would first of all have been understood by the Hebrews in a literal sense—and that means in terms of their conception of the physical world. The light (made, of course, by God as well as called into being by him) comes flooding in upon the darkness of the primaeval chaos and (verse 4) pushes it back. This initiates the cycle of time as (verse 5) the two entities are turned into day and night and allowed by God to invade each other's territory in succession. In this way the darkness in the world is brought under control and given a safe task to perform.

It is interesting that this initial light, now become daylight, is distinguished from the light of the sun, which only comes into existence with the creation of the heavenly bodies on the fourth day. This distinction, to us rather quaint, seems to have been general in the ancient Orient, though the functions of the two kinds of light were so similar that not surprisingly confusion sometimes arose. There are some signs of such a confusion in this chapter, where the language of verses 3 to 5 is partly reproduced in verses 14 to 19. The sense is probably that though day and night were there before the sun, the sun and moon were later assigned the duty of supervising their "behaviour". In addition, however, they and the stars were given the oversight of the natural seasons and the years (and one assumes, the months and the weeks as well). In other words, the time cycle, begun on the first day, is on the fourth day further subdivided and extended.

The straightforward meaning was not only important to the Hebrews because that was the way they believed things happened, but for another reason as well. In the "myths" of surrounding peoples light was a deity or at least the property of a deity like the god of dawn or the sun-god. In this chapter it is, however, completely divested of divinity, as are the sun and the other heavenly bodies. Light, sun, moon, stars—all are but physical things, called into existence by the one true God, fashioned by him, and allotted their roles by him. So matter of factly does Gen. 1 state this that we hardly notice, but the point would not be lost on its first audience.

(v)

For us today, however, the antiquarian science of these verses and their hidden polemic against polytheism fade into the background alongside their symbolic significance.

The Hebrews themselves must have been aware of this just as they were aware of the double layer of meaning in verse 2. Consider the Psalmist's

> For with thee is the fountain of life;
>   in thy light do we see light.

(Ps. 36:9)

or his

> For thou hast delivered my soul from death,
>   yea, my feet from falling,
> that I may walk before God
>   in the light of life.

(Ps. 56:13)

As the Hebrews looked out on the physical world to which they belonged, they could not help fearing the dark and threatening chaos of water and desolation behind its ordered exterior. But they read the signs of a similar conflict in the spiritual universe also. They knew that God in his providence had built into the very fabric of existence a dualism of light and darkness, life and death.

So did the New Testament. The Prologue to John's Gospel, for instance, is nothing other than a rewriting of Genesis

Chapter 1 with the mission of Jesus Christ in the centre of the stage. He becomes God's creating Word, and with his Incarnation a new light of life breaks in upon a world in the grip of evil. That light can be seen shining amid the darkness of chaos, and it is the New Testament's faith that "the darkness has not overcome it" or, as Dr. William Barclay renders it, "did not put it out" (John 1:5).

John Ellerton also knew the truth of this when he wrote in his morning hymn:

> This is the day of light:
>   Let there be light today;
> O Dayspring, rise upon our night,
>   And chase its gloom away.
>
> This is first of days:
>   Send forth thy quickening breath,
> And wake dead souls to love and praise,
>   O Vanquisher of death.

Who are we to say that he is not in his poetic way penetrating to the abiding meaning of Creation's first day?


## THE FIRST OF DAYS—AND GOD SAW THAT IT WAS GOOD

Genesis 1:3–5 (*cont'd*)

### (vi)

*And God saw that the light was good.* God expressed his satisfaction with a job well done. He did the same after his other creative acts (verses 10, 12, 18, 21, 25). And at the end of the chapter, before retiring to his Sabbath rest, he gave his retrospective judgment on the whole process. "And God saw everything that he had made, and behold, it was very good" (verse 31).

To the Hebrews this unvarnished verdict buttressed their faith that the world in which they lived began with and continued to exist due to the consistent and beneficent will of a single good God. Other nations parcelled the world out among a multiplicity of deities, some good, some nasty, and were never sure where they stood. The characteristic mood of their religions was resignation. The Hebrews were no easy optimists. The light in their world was matched by a darkness which in this very verse (4) is expressly not called good. They knew only too well that darkness and chaos were never far away, but they were also convinced that only one God—their God—was in control. Because of that the characteristic mood of their religion was hope. There was room amid life's enigmas and disasters for happiness and joy. This world in which God had set them was a good place, and life was to be welcomed and enjoyed.

There have been times in the history of the Church when Christians have turned from the world and regarded material and fleshly things as tainted and sinful. There is not the slightest warrant in this chapter for such an attitude.

The life of this world matters to God and it should matter to us too. There is so much suffering in it, so much deprivation, so much greed and selfishness, so much profligate waste, so much destruction of its wildlife, so much despoiling of its natural resources that it is almost obscene in this day and age to disengage ourselves from the struggle to make it better and settle for the salvation of our own souls. That does not mean that we should place our trust in any illusory earthly utopia of human devising. That would be to go to the opposite extreme. What is needed is a sane and realistic Old Testament attitude to the world that neither denigrates it nor exalts it. For it is God's world and it is where for the time being God has put us and where for the time being our duty lies.

### (vii)

Let us therefore accept its good gifts gratefully, let us enjoy its beauty and marvel at its complexity, and let us not get so downhearted that we despair of it more than its Creator does. It is still recognizable as God's good Creation, and it is still incumbent upon us, as his creatures, to praise and magnify him who "made all things well". He is in charge and we are free to relax and to rejoice.

The poet of Psalm 104 (a Psalm which could almost be regarded as a poetic version of this chapter) struck the right note when he said of God's "manifold works":

These all look to thee,
  To give them their food in due season.
When thou givest to them, they gather it up;
  when thou openest thy hand, they are filled with good things.
When thou hidest thy face, they are dismayed;
  when thou takest away their breath, they die
  and return to their dust.
When thou sendest forth thy Spirit, they are created;
  and thou renewest the face of the ground.
May the glory of the Lord endure for ever,
  may the Lord rejoice in his works,
Who looks on the earth and it trembles,
  who touches the mountains and they smoke!
I will sing to the Lord as long as I live;
  I will sing praise to my God while I have being.

(Ps. 104:27–33)

So did Francis of Assisi, a saint who knew more than most the suffering of the world and more than most laboured to relieve it. We can only try to emulate his wonderful sense of the goodness of all Creation, and take to ourselves the advice he gave to his followers: "Let us leave sadness to the Devil and his angels. As for us, what can we be but rejoicing and glad?"

## THE FIRST OF DAYS—AND GOD CALLED

Genesis 1:3–5 (*cont'd*)

### (viii)

*God called the light Day*. After creating the light and separating it from the darkness, God assigns names to the two of them. So on the second day with the firmament (verse 8) and on the third day with the earth and the seas (verse 10). We have here again a very Hebraic mode of expression. For the Hebrews to name something was not only to identify it but (almost like a magic

spell) had connotations of exercising power over it. That is the
reason why they would not take the divine name (probably
pronounced "Yahweh") on their lips, but wherever they met it
in the sacred text said instead *Adonai* "The Lord". It was in
their eyes too much like forcing their will on God. But here, of
course, it is God who is doing the naming. He it is who rightfully
assigns everything its place and disposes of everything as he sees
fit.

> He determines the number of the stars,
> he gives to all of them their names.

(Ps. 147:4)

> I have called you by name, you are mine.

(Isa. 43:1)

It is worth noting that when we come to the fourth day, the
sun and the moon are not given their ordinary names but are
described (verse 16) in circumlocution as the greater light and
the lesser light. This is not at all to suggest that God did not
control them in exactly the same way as he controlled the light,
the heavens, the earth and the seas. Exactly the opposite is the
case. The everyday names of the sun and the moon were among
Israel's neighbours also the names of the deities they represented. So this time by *not* using their names the author is in his
own subtle way giving them their proper place in the true God's
scheme of things, and he is as well putting the false gods of the
nations firmly in *their* place.

### (ix)

At the end of this infinitely rich passage describing the first day
of Creation we have the sentence, "And there was evening and
there was morning, one day." This sentence, which occurs with
a different number at the close of each of the paragraphs
dealing with the other days of Creation (verses 8, 13, 19, 23, 31),
has sometimes been taken to indicate that for the Hebrews the
day (in its extended sense equivalent to our twenty-four hours)
began at sunset. I am sure this is a wrong interpretation, which
unnecessarily complicates the issue.

We have just had described God's work on the first day which, if we may so put it, must have been carried out during the hours of daylight. That done, the verse records the onset of evening and, after the intervening night, of the next morning. At that juncture the first full "twenty-four hours" of Creation are over, and the second day begins with God's second speech, "Let there be a firmament . . . ." It is to our way of thinking a rather curious way of putting it, but it is as straightforward as that.

## ON MATTERS OF STYLE AND STRUCTURE

Genesis 1:6–25

After the separation of light and darkness on the first day, which is God's first creative act, the story proceeds:

*Second day, second creative act* (1:6–8)

And God said, "Let there be a firmament in the midst of the waters, and let it separate the waters from the waters." And God made the firmament and separated the waters which were under the firmament from the waters which were above the firmament. And it was so. And God called the firmament Heaven.

And there was evening and there was morning, a second day.

*Third day, third and fourth creative acts* (1:9–13)

And God said, "Let the waters under the heavens be gathered together into one place, and let the dry land appear." And it was so. God called the dry land Earth, and the waters that were gathered together he called Seas. And God saw that it was good.

And God said, "Let the earth put forth vegetation, plants yielding seed, and fruit trees bearing fruit in which is their seed, each according to its kind, upon the earth." And it was so. The earth brought forth vegetation, plants.yielding seed according to their own kinds, and trees bearing fruit in which is their seed, each according to its kind. And God saw that it was good.

And there was evening and there was morning, a third day.

*Fourth day, fifth creative act* (1:14–19)

And God said, "Let there be lights in the firmament of the heavens to separate the day from the night; and let them be for signs and for seasons and for days and years, and let them be lights in the firmament of the heavens to give light upon the earth." And it was so. And God made the two great lights, the greater light to rule the day, and the lesser light to rule the night; he made the stars also. And God set them in the firmament of the heavens to give light upon the earth, to rule over the day and over the night, and to separate the light from the darkness. And God saw that it was good.

And there was evening and there was morning, a fourth day.

### *Fifth day, sixth creative act* (1:20-23)

And God said, "Let the waters bring forth swarms of living creatures, and let birds fly above the earth across the firmament of the heavens." So God created the great sea monsters and every living creature that moves, with which the waters swarm, according to their kinds, and every winged bird according to its kind. And God saw that it was good. And God blessed them, saying, "Be fruitful and multiply and fill the waters in the seas, and let birds multiply on the earth."

And there was evening and there was morning, a fifth day.

### *Sixth day, seventh and eighth creative acts* (1:24–31)

And God said, "Let the earth bring forth living creatures according to their kinds: cattle and creeping things and beasts of the earth according to their kinds." And it was so. And God made the beasts of the earth according to their kinds and the cattle according to their kinds, and everything that creeps upon the ground according to its kind. And God saw that it was good.

There follows in verses 26–31 the eighth creative act (the creation of "man") and the conclusion of the sixth day, and in 2:1–3 the account of the seventh day (the Sabbath).

One of the things which soon strikes us about this chapter is how many of the phrases we met in verses 3–5 are repeated again and again throughout it. It is well worth our while considering the implications of this more fully. The whole story of Creation is in fact written in a very distinctive and sonorous style and is given a plot structure that is almost breathtaking in its architectural simplicity. There must be more to this than mere artistic skill. I believe that both the style and the structure conceal exceptionally valuable clues about the author's purpose in composing it and the meaning he wants us to take from it.

(i)

If modern scholarship is right in assigning this chapter to the document denoted by the letter "P", our author was probably a priest and a bit of an academic and recluse. We catch the flavour of the "priestly" style best by reading through a book like Leviticus and savouring its obvious and loving concern for the sacred laws and institutions of Israel. Leviticus may not be our favourite book of the Bible, but we have to admire the restraint and dignity of its language, its painstaking eye for detail, its studious definitions, even its use of repetition to make its points.

Genesis Chapter 1 shows many of these same features. It is cool and circumspect, sometimes cryptic, and it frequently repeats itself. In our earlier comments we have already compared it a few times with a more popular Hebrew Creation story, which the poets were not afraid to quote and which had God doing battle with the chaos monster Leviathan. We saw that Gen. 1 does not remove the clash between good and evil of which that story spoke, but it will have no truck with a monster and clearly prefers a measure of theological fastidiousness to the vigorous clash of contest.

However, in making such comparisons we should not overdo it. Gen. 1 may have been written by a priest, but it is not for all its coolness an academic composition. We should not forget that it, as much as the more popular Creation story, is an imaginative story, meant to be told to ordinary folks and understood by them. Its style may be austere, but it is not abstruse or pedantic. It is in the best sense of the word a simple style. It can be deceptively simple and if we are not attentive, cause us to miss the profundity of the message. The trouble we had with verse 2 and indeed with some of the phraseology of verses 3–5 is enough to remind us of that. But it is still simple, and it does not lack earthiness.

Our priestly author in short is well aware of what he is doing. He is addressing ordinary folks, and he wishes them to share his vision of God as a God of infinite grace who created a good world for them to live in, and as a saving God who knows the evil to which they are exposed and has moved to control it. But as a priest he wishes above all to show him as a transcendent God, holy and apart, the sovereign Lord of Creation with whom his creatures dare not become too familiar. I think we can agree that he has found a style which beautifully matches both his audience and his subject matter.

(ii)

To an appropriate style the author joins an artistic arrangement of the course of Creation. We have already noted the recurring phraseology, but here we are trying to work out how it is used to make up a structured whole.

Following the setting of the scene in the first two verses there is a dominant structure of *seven* panels, each covering one of seven days and each (except the last) ending with the same sentence giving the day's number. But behind that seven day structure is a second structure of *eight* creative acts of God, each with almost the same pattern of wording, viz.

| | |
|---|---|
| introduction to the command: | *God said* |
| the command: | *Let there be* |
| result of the command: | *And it was so* |
| working out of the command: | *God separated, made,* etc. |
| naming of what is made: | *God called* (first three acts only) |
| classifying of what is made: | *... according to their kinds* (fourth, sixth and seventh acts only) |
| blessing of what is made: | *God blessed* (sixth and eighth acts only) |
| verdict on the result: | *God saw that it was good* |

This second structure is inserted neatly into the first so that there are two creative acts on each of the third and the sixth days. Finally the whole is rounded off with the Sabbath rest of

God on the seventh day, which balances the introduction of verses 1 and 2.

Let us in the following pages look more closely at this arrangement.

## THE HARMONY OF CREATION

Genesis 1:6–25 (*cont'd*)

Firstly we consider the symmetry of the story and in particular the part played in it by the seven day scheme.

### (i)

The symmetry must clearly reflect the author's understanding of the universe as a harmonious whole, ordered by God and sustained by his providence. The eight creative acts are not meant to cover everything in it (wind and rain, for instance, are omitted, as are rivers and springs, and only a few species of plant and animal are listed) but to provide a representative classification of its various parts. The seven day scheme adds the idea of a development in time. There is an unfolding step by step of God's plan until out of chaos cosmos emerges and is filled with his creatures.

### (ii)

The following table gives my reconstruction of the process as I feel the author conceived it. It is presented in four Acts (as in a play) or perhaps better, since the word "act" is rather awkward in the present context, four Movements (as in a symphony). These are indicated by the letters A to D.

A. *The introduction* (verses 1 and 2), which consists of a firm statement that the process was initiated by God, and describes the start of it in terms of a chaos with three constituents—

(a) an earth which is *tohu wa-bohu*
(b) the waters of *tehom*
(c) darkness

B. *The first three days,* during which the constituents of chaos are brought under control in reverse order—

Day 1: Darkness [(c)] by the creation of light. These two entities are given roles as day and night which follow one another, and time begins.

Day 2: The waters [(b)] by the creation of the firmament. The upper portion of the waters is pushed upwards and outwards by the firmament, and space comes into being.

Day 3: The *tohu wa-bohu* [(a)] *first* by the gathering together of the lower portion of the waters, which leads to the emergence of a dry earth, and *second* by the growth of vegetation, which leads to the emergence of a fertile earth.

C. *The second three days,* during which the newly emerged cosmos is organized and filled out in corresponding order—

Day 4: Time (Day 1) by the creation of sun, moon and stars. These oversee a further subdivision of time into seasons and years (and one could add, months and weeks) as well as days.

Day 5: The waters (Day 2) by the creation of fish and birds. These populate the waters and the space which had been inserted in their midst.

Day 6: The earth (Day 3) by the creation *first* of the land animals, which populate it, and *second* of human beings, who are entrusted by God with the governing of it.

D. *The conclusion* (2:1–3). All that was necessary having been accomplished, God rests on the seventh day, retiring into the interior life which six days before he had surrendered in order to begin the process.

## THE DAYS OF CREATION

Genesis 1:6–25 (*cont'd*)

(iii)

A large part of the weight of this artistic structure is carried by the seven day scheme. This scheme was already known to Hebrew tradition, for it figures in the explanation attached to the fourth commandment (Exod. 20:8–11). We cannot say, however, what kind of popular story accompanied it in that tradition, so we can only make our judgment on the scheme's significance on the basis of the story as we have it in the present chapter. As I see it, the author's purpose with it is not at all what many modern readers have assumed it to be.

(iv)

I am thinking here especially of the commonly expressed opinion that if we understand "day" as equivalent to "epoch" or "era", we can bring the sequence of Creation in the chapter into relationship with the accounts of modern evolutionary theory, and so go some way towards recovering the Bible's reputation in our scientific age. The opinion is usually supported by a reference to Ps. 90:4—

> A thousand years in thy sight
> are but as yesterday when it is past,
> or as a watch in the night

—and by detailed comparisons showing how in this or that regard Gen. 1 anticipates the findings of modern science, notably in the watery beginnings of the earth and the precedence of sea creatures over land creatures.

In so far as this argument begins with an attempt to go beyond the literal meaning and to take the week assigned to Creation as a parable of a much longer period, it is to be commended. I am sure that the author is not intending us to think of Creation as something over within a week of its being started. The supercilious school children who, as we mentioned earlier, sneer at Genesis because they assume that the Hebrews read the story as literally as they do are missing the point.

The trouble with the argument we are considering is that having begun with an imaginative interpretation, it too soon misses the point and shows that its real concern is not with the spiritual message of the narrative but with what it regards as the facts of the case. It wants us to conclude that under divine inspiration the author was being given an advance secret knowledge of what has only been discovered in our own day.

This may seem an improvement on the attitude the Church used to adopt in the days when it attacked science as untrue because it did not square with Scripture. But for all its apparent approval of science's findings, it is in essence making the same mistake of regarding the Bible as a scientific textbook.

I must therefore insist once again as strongly as I can that the author of Gen. 1 is not primarily interested in imparting scientific facts, either to his own contemporaries or, in some sort of code, to us. There is nothing on the level of fact in the chapter that an educated Hebrew if not an uneducated one would not already have known. The author accepts the views of the physical world current in his time, and concentrates thereafter on relating these views to his belief in Israel's God as Creator.

If in some respects his story accords with the findings of science, the credit is not therefore his, nor is it the Holy Spirit's, but it is due to ancient scholarship, which in these respects employed accurate observation and speculation. In exactly the same way, it is due to ancient ignorance if in other respects there is a wide gulf between Genesis and science, for example, in its assumption that the sun moves round the earth or that there are vast waters beyond the sky.

(v)

Properly understood, the "days" of Creation are not part at all of the information given in the story but, as I have been suggesting, belong to the techniques the author uses to make his story a good one and suitable for his audience. The seven day scheme is, in short, an aid to the imagination of a simple people. It enabled the Hebrews to take in at one go, as it were, the whole scope and glory of God's work in making the world. It intentionally compressed what even they knew took a long, long time within the compass of a single week, almost as if God were saying as one farmer to another, "That was a good week's stint, was it not?"

In putting it so crudely as that, I am no doubt going beyond what our austere author would have considered appropriate.

But I want to get it across that he is here making use of a very homely metaphor. Far from carping at its down-to-earthness, we who live in a vastly more complicated age than the Hebrews did would do well to think ourselves sympathetically into its symbolism. For where amid the myriad voices of science today, dinning into our ears more and yet more knowledge and theory of astrophysics and geology and biology and anthropology, is it possible to hear a voice that speaks to us so directly and authoritatively of God's grand design for the universe? If there is one, it is lost in the welter of hypothesis, scepticism and prevarication.

For all its scientific primitiveness we still need this old chapter because, in a way that by its very nature science is incapable of matching, it takes us right to the heart of the matter. We will be much the poorer if we are too sophisticated to listen to it in the spirit it was written.

## A STORY FOR CHILDREN?

Genesis 1:6–25 (*cont'd*)

The other feature of the author's arrangement of the story is the *repetitions,* which sound out like hammer blows all through the chapter. We have drawn attention to these several times, but have now to ask what their purpose might be.

(i)

Their cumulative and patently intentional effect is to place God, not the world, squarely in the centre of the stage. Each act of Creation begins, continues, and ends with him. He is there before any of it. Everything is planned by him, and everything works out in accordance with his plan. Even the chaos or evil in the world is assigned its place by him. When it is all over he withdraws to his private rest. No one listening to this story could be in any doubt about the uniqueness of little Israel's God, who it was that created the world by his grace and who it is that rules it by his power.

(ii)

It has sometimes been suggested that Gen. 1 was composed for
solemn recitation during public worship. This is not impossible,
and as well as fitting in with the author's priestly interests would
account nicely for the repetitions. All liturgies tend to be
repetitive. We need think only of the stereotyped pattern of our
own prayers in Church—"O God, who ... be pleased to
... these things we ask through Jesus Christ our Lord, unto
whom ..."

I am, however, more attracted by a recent theory of Father
Sean McEvenue that the chapter has its origin in the education
of children. It seems to me to have the ring of instruction rather
than of formal worship. It reminds us indirectly about our duty
to adore him, but it is telling us about God rather than
addressing him. It is, of course, instruction through the medium
of a story, but is that not the way we still use with children,
because it is the way best suited to them? At any rate, Father
McEvenue has had the happy idea of comparing the chapter
with several well-known nursery rhymes and fairy tales of
European tradition and with a number of more contrived
modern pieces which imitate their way of doing things. In a very
large number of these a patterned repetition is one of the
favourite techniques of the story-teller.

McEvenue himself quotes from "The Little Red Hen" to
illustrate this particular device, but there are many other
examples, for instance the tale of "Chicken Licken". You may
remember how it goes:

Once upon a time there was a little chicken called Chicken Licken.
One day an acorn fell from a tree and hit Chicken Licken on the
head. Chicken Licken thought that the sky was falling down. So he
ran off to tell the King.

On the way, Chicken Licken met Henny Penny. "Good morning,
Chicken Licken," said Henny Penny. "Where are you going in such
a hurry?" "Oh! Henny Penny!" said Chicken Licken. "The sky is
falling down and I'm on my way to tell the King." "Then I'd better go
with you," said Henny Penny. So Chicken Licken and Henny Penny
hurried on, to tell the King that the sky was falling down.

On the way, Chicken Licken and Henny Penny met Cocky Locky. "Good morning, Chicken Licken," said Cocky Locky. "Where are you two going in such a hurry?" "Oh! Cocky Locky!" said Chicken Licken. "The sky is falling down and we are on our way to tell the King." "Then I'd better go with you," said Cocky Locky. So Chicken Licken, Henny Penny and Cocky Locky hurried on, to tell the King that the sky was falling down.

On the way, Chicken Licken, Henny Penny and Cocky Locky met Ducky Lucky. "Good morning, Chicken Licken," said Ducky Lucky. "Where are you all going in such a hurry?" "Oh! Ducky Lucky!" said Chicken Licken. "The sky is falling down and we are on our way to tell the King." "Then I'd better go with you," said Ducky Lucky. So Chicken Licken, Henny Penny, Cocky Locky and Ducky Lucky hurried on, to tell the King that the sky was falling down.

. . . . . .

As the story proceeds, Drakey Lakey, Goosey Loosey and Turkey Lurkey join in, until the birds come upon Foxy Loxy. He tells them that he knows where to find the King, and they all follow him. But he leads them straight to his den, where his wife and their little foxes were waiting for their dinners—

Then the foxes ate Chicken Licken, Henny Penny, Cocky Locky, Ducky Lucky, Drakey Lakey, Goosey Loosey and Turkey Lurkey for their dinners. So Chicken Licken never found the King to tell him that he thought the sky was falling down.

It is not difficult to see why this story has nine or ten panels with a repetition of the same wording within each. The panels are plainly designed to break up the narrative so that the children listening know where they are, and to slow down the flow of information to their speed of comprehension.

(iii)

In suggesting that the panelling structure and repetitions of Gen. 1 may have served a similar end in the education of the young in ancient Israel, Father McEvenue seems to me to be on to something very perceptive. Those of us who have to read stories to little children will know how they adore repetition and how we must make time for it, though we with an adult's taste want to press on and find out what happens next. I wonder, however, if he is being quite perceptive enough. Considering the antiquity of Genesis, might not the story have been intended not simply for Israel's children but for a *childlike Israel?*

I mean this in the best sense. As Father McEvenue himself admits, the difference between adults' and children's taste was once not nearly so wide as it is now. Many of our so-called fairy tales are in fact folk tales of early Europe that used to be enjoyed by adults, but have in our more sophisticated days been relegated to the nursery. I can see no reason why Gen. 1 could not have been composed for the unlettered majority of Hebrews and been (along with many other Biblical tales) told to them by their story-tellers at their various social gatherings, particularly perhaps during the festivities (which included much more than services in a temple building) at the great seasonal pilgrimages like Passover or Tabernacles.

At any rate, thanks to McEvenue's insight we can say with some certainty that the priestly author of this chapter, far from being divorced from common life, is with his patterns of repetition making use of a device which is familiar from the oral tales of many societies and is still widespread in children's literature today.

## GOD'S FREE GRACE

Genesis 1:6–25 (*cont'd*)

### (iv)

There is one further matter worth noticing about the repetitions of Gen. 1, namely that they are not always uniform.

Thus in verse 4 only the light is seen to be good, not God's separating it from the darkness. In the same way God's separation of the waters in verse 7 is not pronounced good. These two omissions probably have a theological reason, and should be connected with the movement from chaos to cosmos to which we drew attention earlier and which lasts from verse 3 to verse 10. In this part of the story the surviving elements of chaos are not in themselves good and the process has to be completed before that judgment can be passed upon it.

But there are other irregularities which cannot be explained in this way. Eight times we have "And God said, Let . . .", but only five times is this answered immediately by the phrase "And it was so". This phrase is omitted altogether after the creation of the fish and the birds on the fifth day (verse 20), and it is shifted to a later place in verses 7 and 30. Again, in verse 9 there is no mention of God carrying out his own command, and in verse 12 where we expect him to be doing it, "the earth" is the subject of the phrase. Another anomaly is the omission of the blessing on the animals (verse 25), although it is pronounced immediately before on the fish and the birds (verse 22) and immediately after on "man" (verse 28). Finally, we may note several irregularities in the lists of the various classes of animals in verses 20–21, 24–25, 26, 28, and 30.

If we were to go by "Chicken Licken", we might be tempted to regularize the text by restoring omissions or moving phrases to their "proper" places, especially when we discover that in some cases the ancient Greek version, the Septuagint, does just that. We should probably resist the temptation. It may be significant that in the children's literature we have been mentioning, the most exact patterning is found in modern artificial stories like "The Little Red Hen" and "Chicken Licken", not in the more traditional tales. In the latter as in Gen. 1 the storytellers vary their patterns slightly here and there, presumably to avoid monotony. Real traditional literature is, it seems, not so strict as its modern imitators.

(v)

Is it too subtle to suggest that the author of Gen. 1 has another reason still for introducing these small variations, namely to discourage his listeners from thinking that they could ever have God's activity neatly taped? Perhaps he sensed a danger in making everything too uniform and wished, while setting forth

the harmony and order of the divine Creation, to leave room for
the free grace of God to operate, the free grace of him who said
to Moses: "I will be gracious to whom I will be gracious, and
will show mercy to whom I will show mercy" (Exod. 33:19).

I like to think that that was his intention, for it would confirm
that he was as good a theologian as he was a story-teller. It is a
lesson that all who take upon themselves the task of explaining
God's ways with the world and with human beings must learn
early and keep before them at all times (see also the commentary
on 4:3–7).

## ACCORDING TO THEIR KINDS

Genesis 1:6–25 (*cont'd*)

There remain two of the chapter's repeated phrases to be
considered. The first is the specifying of the earth's plant life
and the members of the animal kingdom "according to their
kinds" (verses 11, 12, 21, 24, 25). The second is the blessing
pronounced on the fish and birds (verse 22) and on "man"
(verse 28).

### (i)

The manner in which the earth's flora and fauna are classified is
rather rough and ready. We have a hint of a biological distinction in the division of vegetation into two types (verses 11 and
12), plants like barley and wheat which carry their seeds on the
outside and trees like the fig and olive which enclose them inside
their fruit. On the other hand, in organizing the land animals
(verses 24 and 25) the author seems to rely partly on function,
the domesticated animals (cattle) being distinguished from the
wild animals (beasts of the earth), and partly on size, both of
these as large animals being distinguished from smaller animals
like reptiles and rodents (creeping things, or perhaps more
accurately, "lightly moving" things).

It is clear that precise classification in our sense of the term is not what the author is aiming at. Rather, by insisting that the plants and trees, the fish and the birds, and the earth animals be identified "according to their kinds", he shows that he is interested not only in the grand design of nature but in its every individual member. He is telling us that by creating each, God has given to each a usefulness and a dignity in its own right. Moreover, in spite of what is said later about "man's" rule over the creatures (verses 26 and 28), it is apparent that that usefulness is not necessarily related to "man", and that that dignity is not necessarily dependent on him.

(ii)

We are in touch here with a most remarkable side to the Bible's attitude to nature. The Bible is never sentimental or romantic about nature. In this, as we saw earlier, it is quite different from modern nature-poetry like Wordsworth's. The vastness, the violence, the bountiful provision of nature—these along with its orderliness (as in this chapter) are the aspects which are emphasized most strongly. But if we read with a little more care, there is one other note that is constantly struck—God's providential concern for the more helpless and peculiar and indeed dangerous of his creatures.

I am sure it is an awareness of this that moves the author of Gen. 1 to give a special mention to the nasty creeping things of verses 24 and 25 and that accounts, at least partially, for his allusion in verse 21 to the great "sea monsters". No doubt this name was meant to remind his audience of the "monster" of chaos and evil, variously called Leviathan or Rahab or Behemoth, which they so feared. Having rigorously excluded this monster from his own picture of chaos in verse 2, he feels safe in bringing it in at this juncture, and thus makes the point obliquely once again that chaos and evil are in God's control.

But he surely also wishes to underline that not only the placid fish but the huge and fearsome aquatic beasts like the whale or crocodile or hippopotamus, with which Leviathan and its cousins were sometimes poetically compared (see particularly

Job 40: 15ff. and 41:1ff.), had their own inalienable right to live and move in the waters—inalienable because it was "written in" by God when he made the world.

The place where this lesson comes over more clearly than anywhere else is the great 39th chapter of Job. There the Lord goes over for Job's benefit a list of creatures which seem to have little in common apart from the fact that they live far from the haunts of human beings, or are heedless of their commands, or have ways that are beyond their understanding—the mountain goats who bear their young in the open, the wild ass who scorns the tumult of the city, the wild ox (the AV has "unicorn"!) who cannot be bound in the furrow, the incredibly stupid ostrich who is cruel to her young yet can run faster than the horse, the mighty battle horse who laughs at fear, the soaring hawk and the eagle diving on its prey. We don't actually get the lesson spelled out, but it is obvious. The God whose peculiar providence cares for these creatures cannot be tied down to Job's—or any human—ideas of him. There is more to Creation than the welfare of "man".

But there is also the pelican in the wilderness and the sparrow on the housetop of Ps. 102:6–7 (though the RSV turns them into a vulture and a "lonely bird"!) and the sparrow and swallow of Ps. 84:3 who build their nests even in God's Temple, not to mention the sparrow which does not fall to the ground without our Father's will (Matt. 10:29) or the lilies of the field which God clothes with loveliness, though they soon vanish (Matt. 6:28–30). And there are the "much cattle" of Jon. 4:11, which God wants to spare along with Nineveh's 120,000 human inhabitants. And so we could go on.

I can think of no other literature, ancient or modern—unless it be the writings of St. Francis with their "my little sisters the birds" or "our brother leveret" or even "brother wolf"—where there is such a totally sincere and unsentimental fellow-feeling for the whole of created nature. It must arise from the Hebrews' recognition that everything and everyone beneath the heavens were like themselves God's creatures, even—perhaps especially—the odd and the weak and the repellent. Seen against the background of Scripture this is what emerges as the deepest meaning of the phrase "according to their kinds".

### (iii)

C. S. Lewis has some words about this sympathy of the Hebrews with animals which we would do well to ponder. It is not, he says "our modern kindness to animals. That is a virtue most easily practised by those who have never, tired and hungry, had to work with animals for a bare living, and who inhabit a country where all dangerous wild beasts have been exterminated." Not that he wishes to slight such kindness. Nevertheless, though "we may properly be kicked if we lack it, we must not pat ourselves on the back for having it. When a hard-worked shepherd or carter remains kind to animals, his back may well be patted; not ours."

It was respect that the Hebrews as themselves practically-minded countryfolk gave to the world of nature. And that is what we owe it too. Respect for all animals, not just the ones we like, respect for their dignity, their habits, their right to exist. And the same goes for the many species of plant life which we are constantly and selfishly exploiting. Not more respect than for human beings, but the respect that is their due because God made them.

## AND GOD BLESSED THEM

Genesis 1:6–25 (*cont'd*)

The word "bless" means next to nothing to us. "Bless my soul!" we say when we are surprised. Even in our prayers when we ask God to "bless" us or thank him for his many "blessings", it is merely another way of saying "be good" to us or thank you for the "gifts" you have given us. We have quite lost touch with the special aura of sanctity which surrounds the act of blessing in the Bible. We are thus in danger of missing altogether one of the undoubted high spots in this Creation story.

For the blessing plays an extremely important role in Gen. 1. The great inanimate objects in Creation, the firmament of heaven and the earth and seas, and (by implication) the sun, moon and stars, are *named* by God—and are thus seen to be under his control. The "lower" forms of life like the plants and the "higher" forms like the birds and fish and animals are identified by him *according to their kinds*—and are thus given individual worth and dignity in his scheme of things.

But the "higher" forms of life are singled out for something more, and in this they are joined by "man". The fish and the birds and "man" and (we may presume) the land animals are all *blessed* by God—they are specially equipped by him in a way that nothing else in Creation is. This consists, as the following words in each case make plain, in their ability to propagate their kind, to "be fruitful and multiply" (see *note* following). In a very basic sense they are brought close to divinity. They have delegated to them something of God's own power to create new life. Little wonder that the formulas of blessing are intoned in such solemn language!

(i)

Once again it is amazing how perceptive Gen. 1 is. Just as the "material" earth is seen as a good place because God so saw it, so "animal" nature is not denigrated but blessed. We have here a recognition long before psychologists like Konrad Lorenz thought of it that there is a wealth of behavioural patterns and relationships in the animal world linking it and humanity indissolubly together. For we must not limit the blessing they share with each other too much. It has to do with more than fertility. It embraces not only the process of conception and birth but spills over into the care of the young and the provision of food and shelter, and it involves ultimately the health and prosperity of the whole social group. We are really speaking about God's rules for the continuance of life in his universe.

(ii)

In the last section we learned the lesson of what true kindness to animals means. We have to accord respect, because God himself accords respect, to all God's creatures, not just the ones that attract us. Here we are given further food for thought.

The so-called carnal passions or instincts that unite us to the animals are not something to be despised and which for us to be genuinely "human" we have to abandon. The "beast" in us— our aggressive instincts, our maternal possessiveness, our sexual desires, our territorial jealousy, our hunting impulse— was put there by God. It may have gone sadly awry because of our sin, but it has its purpose. Perhaps if we were to study the animals more we would find out what it is. How rarely do they overstep the bounds of appropriate behaviour! The animals share with human beings the blessing of Creation, and it is difficult to disagree with the conclusion that in their innocence they get a lot more out of it than we do.

### (iii)

A final short word before we reach the climax of the story in the creation of "man". There is something ultra-special about "man". Gen. 1 makes no bones about that and reserves for him some of its most impressive language. But we must not exaggerate it and when we get onto discussing what the phrase "image of God" as applied to human beings may mean, we must not forget that they are but one part of an immensely varied whole which is far larger than they. If they are the ultimate end of Creation, they are by no means its sole end. This chapter is in no doubt about that either. It does not give "man" a separate "day" to himself but makes him share the sixth day with the earth creatures. Half a day out of six is his ration!

Furthermore, we have just seen how closely Gen. 1 binds up humankind with the animals in the blessing which belongs to both of them. And we shall shortly see how the animals—and indeed the earth itself (verse 28)—are intimately involved in what makes "man" so special. We humans have no cause on the basis of this chapter either to feel particularly proud of ourselves or to think that religion concerns only the fate of our little souls. The earth too is the Lord's and all that it contains. It is salutary to keep this in mind as we leave the wider Creation behind us and concentrate on its most illustrious—but also its most devious and untrustworthy—member.

### *A note on the phrase "be fruitful and multiply"*

It is important to emphasize that the phrases "be fruitful and multiply" and "fill" used of the fish and birds in verse 22 and of "man" in verse 28 have nothing essentially to do with the issue of overpopulation which so concerns the world today. Those who argue against "birth-control" should *not* employ these verses in support of their position, nor on the other hand need those who commend it be perturbed because they are in the Bible. It has to be remembered that this chapter is dealing with the "filling" of an as yet *empty* earth, and it ought not to be expected to have anything *directly* to say about a problem which has only come to prominence in the present century. Nor for that matter should any part of the Bible, which was entirely composed in an age when *under*population rather than overpopulation was the danger facing the earth's inhabitants.

This is not to say, of course, that the problem is not an extremely pressing one, which Christian people ought to be laying to heart. But their contribution towards its solution will have to be based on Biblical *principles,* not on Biblical texts. In the context we have just been considering perhaps the fact that on the whole the animals succeed in keeping their numbers in balance with their environments is what we should be thinking about. In the context we are just coming to—the rule of "man" over the world of nature—our responsibility under God for the welfare of all Creation will be the most relevant principle. In other Biblical contexts, again, other principles like the sanctity of human life or the central role of the family in the building up of a healthy society will be more to the fore. But in the end of the day the problem is so far removed from the realities of life in Biblical times that a commentary like this cannot go much further than to warn its readers against comparing those times too directly with our own. Each reader will have to make up his or her own mind on it, and each will have to take a lot more than a few verses of Genesis into account in doing so.

*A note on words for "man" in Hebrew and English*

There are significant differences between Hebrew and English in this vocabulary field. The Hebrew word *adam* means in the great majority of its occurrences *mankind* or *humanity* in general. Only in Chapters 2 and 3 of Genesis where it is tantamount to a proper name for the male partner in the first human pair does it carry a strong masculine nuance. The normal word in Hebrew for *man* in the sense of "male" is *ish* (as for woman it is *ishshah*). *Ish* or its plural are occasionally but very rarely found in the sense of "humanity".

Usage in English is considerably more ambivalent. It possesses comprehensive terms like *human being* or *humanity*, but when referring to the human race as a whole it mostly prefers to use *man* (as indeed in the Old Testament for *adam*) or less frequently *men* or *mankind*. In the case of *man* or *men* we have to rely on the context to tell us whether the terms are being employed to include or to exclude the female sex.

No one commenting on the early chapters of Genesis can help being aware of these different usages, particularly at the present time when many people—by no means all of them women—are becoming increasingly sensitive to the sexist implications of much of our religious language. I attempt in this volume to take account of the problem in the following ways:

(a) Where as in the case of Gen. 1:26ff. and similar Biblical passages I am specifically commenting on Hebrew texts in which the word *adam* is common, I speak in English of *"man"*, using inverted commas.

(b) Where as in the case of Gen. 2–3 the sex distinction is prominent, I speak simply of *man* and *woman*, even though (unusually) the Hebrew has *adam* for the first.

(c) Where in more general comments I am contrasting the human and the divine, I speak as far as I can of *humanity, human beings, people* etc., even though *man* or *mankind* are (or have been till now) commoner in everyday English usage.

I hope that this compromise will be accepted as reasonable both by those who are trying to alert the Churches to this serious issue and by those who have hitherto not thought much about it.

(The even more important problem of the use of excessively "male" language about God is unfortunately not one to which the Old Testament commentator has much to contribute, since in this field Hebrew usage—like English—is resolutely masculine.)

## "MAN"—THE CREATURE OF GOD

Genesis 1:26–31

> Then God said, "Let us make man in our image, after our likeness; and let them have dominion over the fish of the sea, and over the birds of the air, and over the cattle, and over all the earth, and over every creeping thing that creeps upon the earth." So God created man in his own image, in the image of God he created him; male and female he created them. And God blessed them, and God said to them, "Be fruitful and multiply, and fill the earth and subdue it; and have dominion over the fish of the sea and over the birds of the air and over every living thing that moves upon the earth." And God said, "Behold, I have given you every plant yielding seed which is upon the face of all the earth, and every tree with seed in its fruit; you shall have them for food. And to every beast of the earth, and to every bird of the air, and to everything that creeps on the earth, everything that has the breath of life, I have given every green plant for food." And it was so. And God saw everything that he had made, and behold, it was very good.
>
> And there was evening and there was morning, a sixth day.

With this famous passage the story moves into a distinctly different gear. This is signalled by the way in which God involves himself directly in what is done. Where formerly there had been an impersonal "Let there be . . .", we have an intensely personal "Let us make . . ." It is also signalled by the cruel and unfeeling words used to describe "man's" control over the other creatures, as if it were meant to be absolute. But more than anything else, it is signalled by the description of "man" as (in the usual translation) made in God's image and likeness. How boastful and triumphalist all this sounds!

You will recall that in order to illumine a stark verse 1 and an enigmatic verse 2 we turned to other passages in the Old Testament dealing with the themes of Creation and of chaos. It is even more vital that we adopt this method for the present verses. For unless they are seen against the broader Old Testament picture of "man", they are open to the grossest misrepresentation.

(i)

In the Old Testament as a whole "man" does not get a very good press. Indeed, apart from this passage and one other passage in Ps. 8 to which we shall come later, its teaching about "man" is painfully clear and consistent. Time and again and with an abundance of forceful metaphors and images it rubs in the lesson of the creatureliness of "man", his origin in the dust of the ground, his utter distance from God, his complete dependence upon him, the shortness of his days, his life of trouble and sorrow. And that is without even mentioning his sinfulness!

Here are just a few examples:

> Can mortal man be righteous before God?
>     Can a man be pure before his Maker?
> Even in his servants he puts no trust,
>     and his angels he charges with error;
> how much more those who dwell in houses of clay,
>     whose foundation is in the dust,
>     who are crushed before the moth.
>
> (Job 4:17–19)

> Man is born to trouble
>     as the sparks fly upward.
>
> (Job 5:7)

> Hast thou eyes of flesh?
>     Dost thou see as man sees?
> Are thy days as the days of man,
>     or thy years as man's years?
>
> (Job 10:4–5)

> Man born of a woman
>     is of a few days, and full of trouble.
> He comes forth like a flower, and withers;
>     he flees like a shadow, and continues not.
>
> (Job 14:1–2)

> Lord, let me know my end,
>     and what is the measure of my days;
>     let me know how fleeting my life is!

Behold, thou hast made my days as a few handbreadths,
   and my lifetime is as nothing in thy sight.
Surely every man stands as a mere breath!
   Surely man goes about as a shadow!

                     (Ps. 39:4–6)


     Men of low estate are but a breath,
       men of high estate are a delusion;
     in the balances they go up;
       they are together lighter than a breath.

                     (Ps. 62:9)


As a father pities his children,
   so the Lord pities those who fear him.
For he knows our frame;
   he remembers that we are dust.
As for man, his days are like grass;
   he flourishes like a flower of the field;
for the wind passes over it, and it is gone,
   and its place knows it no more.
But the steadfast love of the Lord is from everlasting to everlasting.

                     (Ps. 103:13–17)


The fate of the sons of men and the fate of beasts is the same; as
one dies, so dies the other. They all have the same breath, and man
has no advantage over the beasts; for all is vanity. All go to one
place; all are from the dust, and all turn to dust again.

                     (Eccl. 3:19–20)


     The Egyptians are men, and not God;
       and their horses are flesh, and not spirit.

                     (Isa. 31:3)


     A voice says, "Cry!"
       And I said, "What shall I cry?"
     All flesh is grass,
       and all its beauty is like the flower of the field.
     The grass withers, the flower fades;
       but the word of our God will stand for ever.

                     (Isa. 40:6–8)

> Cursed is the man who trusts in man
> and makes flesh his arm,
> whose heart turns away from the Lord.
> He is like a shrub in the desert,
> and shall not see any good come.

(Jer. 17:5–6)

Finally, there is the other Creation story of Genesis Chapter 2, where in verse 7 we are given a more detailed description of human beginnings than we get in Chapter 1: "The Lord God formed man of dust from the ground, and breathed into his nostrils the breath of life; and man became a living being."

It would be a rash interpreter indeed who claimed that there was anything in the least divine or even impressive about "man" in any of these passages.

(ii)

We see now why it was necessary to point out in the last section that in Gen. 1 as a whole, "man" is put very firmly in his place. In using of him the astounding words it does, this chapter cannot be departing from the general Old Testament estimate of him, but must be taking that estimate for granted and building upon it.

It is a great pity that traditional interpretations of the final part of the chapter have not usually been as aware of this as they ought to have been. Far too often they have looked for some faculty within the nature of "man" to identify with the divine image—his immortal soul, his reasoning capacity, his superior intelligence, his free will, his sense of the moral imperative, his consciousness of self. In so doing they have shown themselves not only to be under the influence of their own humanist environments, classical or modern, which made (and still make) "man" the measure of all things, but to be quite out of touch with Old Testament thinking. In the Old Testament God and God alone is the measure of all things, and it is quite impossible that any Hebrew could have seen anything in "man" as "man" that would merit the title divine.

## "MAN"—THE IMAGE AND LIKENESS OF GOD

Genesis 1:26–31 (*cont'd*)

Let us try, then, to find an explanation of the divine image and likeness that does not move us too far away from that emphasis on the creatureliness of "man" which, as we have just been reminded, is an inseparable element of the Old Testament's view of human nature.

(i)

This is not an easy thing to do. For when we examine other Old Testament passages which use the words "image" and "likeness" in connection with God—and there are quite a few— Gen. 1:26ff. does seem to stand out like a sore thumb.

The most obvious (to an English reader) is the second commandment, "You shall not make for yourself a graven image, or any likeness . . ." (Exod. 20:4). Unfortunately, neither of the Hebrew nouns in Exodus is the same as the ones in Genesis, so we can hardly say that a Hebrew audience would immediately have thought of the commandment. However, we probably ought not to make too much of this. The words in Exodus are not so different that at a stretch the author of Gen. 1 could not have used them, and equally the Genesis words would not have been all that out of place in the commandment. So if the second commandment did not immediately come into the original audience's mind, it might well have done very soon afterwards.

But even if it didn't, the words in Genesis by themselves would be quite enough to make what the author was saying sound to them rather too near to idolatry for comfort.

The significant fact about the word "image" (Hebrew *tselem*) is that in most of its occurrences in the Old Testament it refers to pagan idols, the actual blocks of wood or stone or metal that were given the shape the Babylonians or Canaanites or Israel's other neighbours thought their gods had. Examples are Num. 33:52 of the gods of Canaan; 2 Kings 11:18 of Baal; Amos 5:26

of unknown gods worshipped alongside the Lord in the corrupt shrine at Samaria. What, his audience would be bound to ask, could the author be getting at in using such a word about the God of Israel?

Their feeling of unease could only have increased when they heard the word "image" followed by the word "likeness" (Hebrew *demuth*).

The significant passages here are to be found in Ezekiel and "Second Isaiah".

The word "likeness" occurs no less than ten times in the remarkable first chapter of Ezekiel, where the prophet is attempting to put into words his experience of being commissioned by God. Everything he sees in his vision is heavily qualified by being prefaced by the phrases "the likeness of" or "the appearance of", including the four Cherubim, the wheels within wheels, a throne, and on the throne (verse 26) "a likeness as it were of a human form". "Such," he concludes (verse 28), "was the appearance of the likeness of the glory of the Lord." To Ezekiel God's presence could not be portrayed but only hinted at. Even a word like "likeness" was too strong to be used on its own.

The prophet of the Exile, warning his fellow exiles against idol worship, was rather more explicit—God had no "likeness" at all.

> To whom then will you liken God,
>   or what likeness compare with him?
> The idol! a workman casts it,
>   and a goldsmith overlays it with gold,
>   and casts for it silver chains.

(Isa. 40:18–19)

With connotations such as those attaching to it, it is obvious that the first hearers of this story would have been just as perturbed at the word "likeness" as at the word "image". How could a Hebrew author—and a priest at that—use these dangerous words in speaking about humanity's relationship with God?

(ii)

There seems to me to be only one way out of this dilemma.

In describing "man" as created "in the image of God" (or—in this context a better translation—"*as* the image of God") and "after his likeness", the author of Gen. 1 must intentionally have been indulging in irony. He was using words that for nine-tenths of their meaning were demonstrably inappropriate to any point he could possibly wish to make. His purpose then must have been to highlight for his audience the small part of their meaning that was appropriate. We have to assume that after their initial shock they, being Hebrews, would be sufficiently on his wave-length to get his message. Can we say the same for ourselves?

Let me attempt a paraphrase. As I see it, the author is, in the most pungent and arresting manner he could think of, trying to say two things about "man"—

(a) He says first: "You know that to those foolish enough to bow down before it, an idol represents a non-existent pagan god. Well, the one true God has—if you will pardon the word— his 'image' too, only that image is not a block of stone but we human beings. We represent him on earth. But we are not, of course, blocks of stone. We represent him not just by being there, but by what we do to help him."

(b) Then he says: "You know that we cannot really describe God, but that we often speak about him in human terms, as though he did in fact talk to us, ask us to do things, was pleased or angry with us, and so on. In that limited sense you could say he is 'like' us, is a 'person'. Well, in exactly the same limited sense we human beings are made 'after his likeness'. We alone in his Creation can talk to him, hear him speaking to us, obey him or disobey him—in short, respond to him. In his grace he has so made us that we *can* be his representatives."

(iii)

If that is a correct interpretation of what Gen. 1:26 is getting at, we begin to understand why the author took such care in formulating it. On the one hand, "man" is God's mere creature just like any other of his creatures, with all that that implies. The author has not the slightest desire to dispute that. On the other hand, he is writing a comprehensive account of Creation, which was not the intention of the authors of the other passages about "man" we quoted some pages ago. He has to say something about "man's" place in the created order as a whole. At this level he wishes to make it clear that "man" had been chosen by God to fill a role in his purposes for the world that no other creature could fill. And it must follow from this that God had established with this creature alone the kind of "personal" relationship that would enable him to get through to him and communicate his will to him. The author's problem is how to get this second stupendous truth across to his audience without compromising the first truth. His solution is to doctor his language with a good dose of irony.

In that way he not only magnifies God's amazing grace in assigning so high a rank to such a creature but at the same time does not let us forget the tremendous risk God took in so doing. To have said nothing at this stage of his story about "man's" very special status in Creation would have left it totally incomplete. To have set forth that status as the grand climax of Creation without introducing a strong hint of paradox would have been to give free rein to "man's" presumption and arrogance. So he chooses words to describe "man" that by their very incongruousness he hopes will aid his audience to form a balanced picture.

I suggest the following rather full translation of the first part of Gen. 1:26: "Then God said, Let us make man (to act) as our representative (on earth), (to be) someone (enough) like ourselves (to be able to understand what we were about in creating the world)." We have now to see how the second part of the verse fits in with this.

## "MAN"—THE VICEROY OF GOD

Genesis 1:26–31 (*cont'd*)

In a famous article appearing in the periodical *Science* in

1967 and entitled "The historical roots of our ecological crisis", Professor Lynn White Jr. of the University of California in Los Angeles traces the superiority of western science and technology to the victory of Christianity over paganism in mediaeval Europe. Its preachers and theologians emptied the natural world of the protecting spirits which the old pagans had always sought to placate before, for example, cutting down a tree or damming a brook, and so freed it for exploitation. Their converts took full advantage. With the verses we are studying ringing in their ears they set out to conquer the earth. God, the Bible told them, had planned the whole universe explicitly for "man's" benefit and for "man's" rule. Made of clay he might be, but he was not simply part of nature, but set above it, created in God's image; and he was invited, nay encouraged, in God's name to subdue the earth and have dominion over all living things.

There is, Professor White is saying, an appalling indifference to the things of nature in the soul of the scientific West which leads it to exploit them unmercifully, and for this situation Christianity and by implication the author of Genesis Chapter 1 must bear a huge burden of responsibility.

Historically considered, the Judeo-Christian view of "man"—or at any rate this aspect of it which sees him as lord of Creation—is by far Christianity's most potent legacy to the world. The modern West has now largely given up the Christian idea of God, but Christian attitudes towards "man's" relation to nature are still universally held. "Despite Copernicus, all the cosmos rotates around our little globe. Despite Darwin, we are *not,* in our hearts, part of the natural process. We are superior to nature, contemptuous of it, willing to use it for our slightest whim."

(i)

This is a scarifying indictment, made all the more so by the fact that Professor White is himself a practising Christian. It contains far too much truth for any who call themselves Christians to do other than shrink in horror from it. Look at the

Christian lands and the erstwhile Christian lands like Communist Russia, and look at the lands where other religions are followed. Which of the two are devouring the earth's oil and its other natural resources at obscene speed, which have long since levelled *their* forests and cleared them of wild animals, which are sleek and fat as they eat more than their share of nature's bounty and which go hungry? Japan may appear to be an exception, but it is not. Its industrial achievements have been built purely on borrowed western know-how and owe nothing to its traditional faith.

The evidence is plain for all to see. Christianity and Genesis, it does seem, have a lot to answer for.

(ii)

But of course what Professor White is describing, though a very real Christianity, is a debased and adulterated Christianity. And the triumphalist understanding of Genesis to which this Christianity is partial is an utterly false understanding.

I have been at pains to labour this many times over in the last dozen pages or more. According to this chapter, properly understood—and that means as the Hebrews understood it—all the earth's creatures and all its plants have their inalienable dignity in God's eyes, and they ought therefore to have it in ours. This chapter sees clearly the unbreakable ties binding the human race and the animal kingdom together, and so therefore should we. This chapter shares the very low estimate of "man" that the rest of the Old Testament has, and does not for an instant challenge the basic belief of the whole Old Testament that only God is the measure of all things; and neither therefore should we. Above all, it uses the word "image" ironically. When the cards are down, it puts "man" unhesitatingly where he belongs, and that is beside his fellow creatures, not beside his Creator.

If at the same time it accords "man" a special status in Creation, it insists that it is a delegated status, not something inherent in his nature. "Man" is God's representative on earth, his ambassador, and possesses no intrinsic rights or privileges beyond those conferred on him by his divine Master, to whom moreover he has to render account. It is not Genesis' fault if Christian theology has torn these verses from their context and read into them what is not there, setting "man" on a pedestal and so—whether unwittingly or not—unleashing the tempest of disaster which Professor White so eloquently describes.

(iii)

How then are we to interpret the harsh verbs in which in the second half of verse 26 and in verse 28 "man's" rule over the world of nature is spelt out? Or more to the point, what would a Hebrew audience have made of them?

The first verb, Hebrew *radah*, in the RSV "have dominion", is much stronger than merely "to rule" (NEB) or even "to master" (Moffatt). It is used in 1 Kings 9:23 of Solomon's overseers levying the forced labour needed to build the Temple and his own palace. Even more appositely, it is used in Isa. 14:2 of Israel defeating her oppressors and turning the tables on them. "Dominate" or "lord it over" would be more accurate English equivalents.

The second verb, Hebrew *kabash*, translated "subdue", means literally "to trample on". It is used in Zech. 9:15 of Israel treading down in the last days the weapons (or the soldiery) of her vanquished enemies. And it is used in Jer. 34:11 of the burghers of Jerusalem grabbing back their slaves after having released them during the Babylonian invasion of Judah. "Subjugate" has the correct nasty nuance.

A sensitive Hebrew would immediately see what the author was driving at. He would recall the very similar verses about "man" in Ps. 8:6–8—

> Thou hast given him dominion over the work of thy hands;
> thou hast put all things under his feet—

and how just before that the Psalmist speaks of God *crowning* "man" with glory and honour. The verbs belonged to the vocabulary of *kingship*. They were autocratic, imperialist verbs. But the generality of human beings were not kings. And in this context only God was King, King of the universe. Only he had absolute power over his creatures.

Nor would he forget that a little earlier still the Psalmist had expressed his utter incredulity at God promoting such a creature to such a position (verse 3 and 4):

> When I look at thy heavens, the work of thy fingers,
> the moon and the stars which thou hast established;
> what is man that thou art mindful of him,
> and the son of man that thou dost care for him?

These verses in Genesis could not possibly have been taken by their first hearers to suggest that "man" could do what he liked with God's Creation. In conjunction with the word "image" they had to be emphasizing that such power as he possessed over it had been given him by God, and that he exercised it in God's place, as his *viceroy*. It is described in a typically Jewish hyperbole as the power of a despot over his subjects or of a taskmaster over his slaves because it is ultimately God's power. "Man" could only use it rightly if he used it as God himself (not some human dictator) would have used it.

(iv)

What a tragedy that this part of Genesis has been read so straightfacedly by western Christendom and that the paradox and exaggeration—the humour even—with which it is invested in the original Hebrew have gone completely unperceived! It has fired the arrogance and ambition of the peoples of the West when in fact it should have done the very opposite. And it has done it so thoroughly that a historian like Professor White, though a believer, is simply unaware that any other interpretation than a triumphalist one is possible.

The Professor ends his paper by calling for an "alternative Christian view" of "man's" standing *vis-à-vis* nature. He himself proposes St. Francis of Assisi as a worthier model, "the greatest radical in Christian history since Christ". He writes: "The key to an understanding of Francis is his belief in the virtue of humility—not merely for the individual but for man as a species. Francis tried to depose man from his monarchy over creation and set up a democracy of all God's creatures."

But Saint Francis ought not to be set over against Genesis Chapter 1. I have already myself quoted him twice to illumine it. They are in their different ways saying the same thing. Long before the mediaeval saint lived his exemplary life the first chapter of God's Word laid down the ideal blueprint for a fairer and juster and happier world. Let what it says get a hearing and the ecological crisis—and many of humanity's other crises as well—will disappear.


## LET US MAKE...

Genesis 1:26–31 (*cont'd*)

Before we leave verse 26 something ought to be said about the peculiar first person plural "us" and "our" used by God of himself here and only here in the chapter (in verses 29 and 30 he reverts to the singular "I"). This used to be taken by the Church Fathers as a hidden reference to the Christian Trinity working in Creation (the Second Person being the creating Word that speaks throughout, and the Third Person the Spirit of verse 2)—but what could the ancient Hebrews have known about these things? Nowadays it is more often compared to the royal or the editorial "we"—but that is a European not a Hebrew idiom. But if it is not to be explained in either of these ways, what does it signify?

### (i)

The parallel passage in Psalm 8 again helps us here. Where in verse 5 it speaks of God "crowning" "man" it also says, "Thou hast made him a little less than God," or as the AV has it, "a little lower than the angels". The Hebrew is in fact *Elohim,* the regular word for God which, as every student of the Bible knows, is itself a plural. It must survive in Hebrew from an earlier stage when Israel's ancestors worshipped many gods and goddesses like their neighbours, and have been retained after they became monotheists because it was a useful reminder to them that what to others were many deities, divided and often squabbling, was now to them a single deity consistent in his will and purposes.

However, there are a few places in the Old Testament where it is still a plural. Most of these are references to actual foreign deities, as in Exod. 12:12 to the gods of the Egyptians, or in Ps. 95:3, "The Lord is a great God [*Elohim*], and a great King above all gods [also *Elohim*]", or even in the first commandment (Exod. 20:3), "You shall have no other gods before me." But very occasionally the reference is to divine beings connected with the God of Israel. A good example is Ps. 138:1, "before the gods I sing thy praise."

To these should be added several allusions to beings called the "sons of God". Examples are Gen. 6:2 (a passage that will cause us some trouble later) and Job 1:6 and 2:1, where the "sons of God" present themselves before the Lord.

We have in such passages another survival from paganism, the idea of the divine council or assembly familiar to us from Homer, where the gods and goddesses gather from time to time to discuss important matters. An example from nearer Israel is the epic of Atrahasis, which contains one of the Mesopotamian versions of the Flood story. It begins with meetings of the divine council where first the gods decide to create human beings to be their slaves (incidentally how different that is from this chapter!) and later decide to destroy them when their din and clamour keep them awake at night (see further the commentary on 6:5–9:19, *The Mesopotamian story of the Flood*).

But in Hebrew thinking such "gods" are (with the possible exception of the perturbing passage in Gen. 6:2 just mentioned) never allowed to threaten the oneness or majesty of the true God. They are not strictly speaking "angels", who are God's messengers, a rank below, as it were, nor are they the Cherubim and Seraphim of other Old Testament passages (e.g. Gen. 3:24; Isa. 6:2), who are God's guardians or ministers. But their role is not greatly different. They are essentially figures of the Hebrew imagination, not personalities in their own right, but mere extensions of God, serving poetically to enhance his glory and holiness and safeguarding rather than challenging his transcendence.

(ii)

Against this background I believe the AV to be much nearer the mark with its "angels" in Ps. 8:5 than the RSV with its "God" with a capital letter. The Psalmist like the author of Gen. 1 wishes to accord "man" a high status, and he pictures it as almost as high as that of the divine beings around God's throne in heaven. In this he goes more than a step—as does Gen. 1:26—beyond the characteristic Old Testament view of "man". But he does not go as far—would any Hebrew?—as to bring "man" into direct comparison with the one holy God himself. Even if he were a "little less than God", he would still be too near God for Hebrew taste.

The use of "us" and "our" in the present verse has surely to be similarly explained. The author of Gen. 1 normally doesn't like poetic language in describing God, as we have had cause to notice on not a few occasions. But here he makes an exception. And the reason he makes an exception is not far to seek. He is alerting his audience to the riskiness of what he is about to say about "man". So he intentionally raises a vision of the heavenly court and conceals God there among his angels for a moment. In that way he distances him just that bit more from "man", and prepares his audience for a properly balanced appreciation of the amazing phrases to follow.

When we consider what later ages have made of Gen. 1:26, and at what theological cost, it is tempting to conclude that the author has not succeeded very well in his intention. But how was he to know that his carefully honed and calculated statements would get into the hands of people so insensitive to the nuances of the Hebrew language?

### A note on the "image" in the New Testament

The doctrine of "man" as the divinely appointed ruler of nature is only one strain in Christian thinking about the *imago dei*. There is another (and largely contradictory) strain which speaks of God's image being obliterated at the Fall and restored in Christ, who alone is the true "image" of the Father. See Rom. 8:29; 1 Cor. 15:49; 2 Cor. 3:18; Eph. 4:24; Col. 1:15; 3:10; Heb. 1:3. This line of thinking also seems at first glance to have connections with Genesis Chapter 1, but it is in reality far more dependent on the conviction of the early Christians that Jesus was the perfect "man", and that other human beings could only hope to attain perfection as they conformed themselves to him. Not for a moment would I wish to question the truth of that insight. But I must point out that it is a highly original Christian development of the idea of the divine "image". We ought not to read it into Genesis.

In Genesis, as 9:6 makes clear, the "image" was *not* effaced at the Fall, or as we should perhaps now rephrase it, "man's" status as God's representative or viceroy was not affected by the fact that he is a sinner who does not merit it. It is because of that status that "man's" blood must not be shed. The underlying thought here is not, of course, that "man" is divine, but of the inviolability of an ambassador's person. Just as relations between states would collapse if they did not respect each other's diplomats, so there could be no progress in divine-human relations if human beings had less respect for one another than God had (see further the commentary on 8:21–22; 9:1–17, *Our God is a consuming fire*).

## MALE AND FEMALE

### Genesis 1:26–31 (*cont'd*)

All the living creatures were created male and female, but the author of Gen. 1 only brings in the distinction at this point (verse 27) where his subject is humanity. He must have had a special reason or reasons for doing this. He doesn't say what they are, but one at least is pretty obvious.

(i)

At the level of the "image" men and women are *equal*. It is not at all unlikely that the author knew the more popular story preserved in Chapter 2, which has woman created after man and is, by himself having them created in the same divine act, implicitly criticizing it. This does not mean that he was thinking of equal political rights for women. That was simply not a live option in his day. But he does inescapably associate women with men in humanity's task of "ruling" the other members of Creation, for that is what to him the "image" is all about.

Perhaps he felt that the kingly and dictatorial terms in which he had described the image were too "masculine" in their flavour and wished to stress the more "motherly" virtues which humanity as a whole should be bringing to this task. If he did, then few later theologians have paid much attention to him, for women have usually been rigorously excluded from anything to do with ruling in the Church.

Far too often the attitude of St. Paul has prevailed. Everyone knows that he didn't consider it proper for women to uncover their heads in church, a relatively minor matter, one would have thought. But look at the reason he gives (1 Cor. 11:7)—that "man is the image and glory of God" and woman only "the glory of man"! This must surely be rejected as quite unworthy, whether it is in the Bible or not. It not only brings a huge theological hammer to crack a tiny social nut, but makes a travesty of this verse in Genesis.

That on the whole the Church has treated women far more kindly than secular society may be true, but it has still a long way to go before it measures up to the standard of Gen. 1:27, where male and female together are appointed as God's representatives and ambassadors to tend his Creation for him and teach it to glorify its Creator. It is both a scandal and an impoverishment of its witness that in many parts of it women are still barred from the ministry or the priesthood. For until the Church puts its own house in order in this regard, it cannot hope to influence the wider world outside to give women their rightful place in humanity's search for peace and justice on this earth. Little wonder, perhaps, that our search has so far been so desultory!

(ii)

If there is another reason why both the male and female are

explicitly brought within the scope of the *imago dei,* it is to underline to the Hebrews that sex was a sacred thing and was not to be degraded by them in the way their Canaanite neighbours degraded it.

Canaanite religion as we know it from the tablets discovered at Ras Shamra in Syria, the ancient Ugarit, was obsessed with the fertility of the soil, and this obsession often spilled over into an obsession with human fertility. Sacred prostitutes were kept at Canaanite sanctuaries to unite with priests in rituals of "sympathetic" magic aimed at ensuring abundant harvests and large families, and in not a few Canaanite religious stories gods and goddesses are depicted copulating freely.

I have myself made a special study of the Ugaritic tablets and have published a critical edition of them, in which I take other scholars to task for too readily assuming that the religion of Canaan was solely concerned with sex and fertility. But there is no doubt that many of its practices were offensive and quite unacceptable to Israel's faith and ethics, and that her prophets were right to warn the Hebrews against having anything to do with them. The "high hills" and "green trees" (Jer. 3:6) where Israel was tempted "to play the harlot" were a real challenge to the purity of her faith, and what went on upon and under them demeaned the proper ends for which Israel's God intended the sexual act.

There is a hidden lesson here too for our modern age. How ironic it is that just when "Women's Lib." movements are gathering increasing momentum, today's versions of the Canaanites' "high hills" and "green trees" are summoning society to worship again at the altar of false and perverted sex! Are women going to advance to freedom and retreat to degradation at the same time?

## I HAVE GIVEN EVERY GREEN PLANT

Genesis 1:26–31 (*cont'd*)

Verses 29 and 30 describe God's provision for the human

beings and animals he had created. We miss the point of them
completely if we take them historically or engage in argument
about whether God meant us to be vegetarians. We may choose
to go on a vegetarian diet, but are we going to force our cats and
dogs to do the same? We have to read them symbolically.

(i)

There is no doubt that the author is in this chapter describing
an actual good world which God created. It is not a fallen
material world which men and women should be intent on
avoiding until the day when their souls finally escape from it
into a higher spiritual realm. It is the everyday world in which
they live their everyday lives, and which they ought to accept
gratefully and enjoy gladly.

Or rather it has been up till this point. Towards the end of the
story we are being given increasingly frequent hints that for all
its goodness, it is not as it was meant by God to be. In the verses
about the "image" there is an implication that "man" as God's
viceroy is in fact not fulfilling his task at all successfully. And in
these verses it is implied that all God's creatures should be at
peace and in harmony with one another and with "man". It
seems to me that the author is suggesting obliquely that there is
something in "man" that for all his powers and abilities causes
him to make a mess of things, and that the animals suffer
because of it as well as himself. For he knew very well that
human beings eat animal flesh and that the animals hunt and
devour each other, and that there never was a time when they
did not.

(ii)

The prophet Isaiah was also very well aware that "man" and the
animals had always engaged in internecine strife, yet when he
painted a picture of what things would be like when the Messiah
came, he said:

> The wolf shall dwell with the lamb,
>   and the leopard shall lie down with the kid,
> and the calf and the lion and the fatling together,

> and a little child shall lead them.
> The cow and the bear shall feed;
>   their young shall lie down together;
>   and the lion shall eat straw like the ox.

(Isa. 11:6–7)

It is obvious that he is taking what we call "nature red in tooth and claw" as representing the way of the present unredeemed world, and is using its opposite, an imagined "Paradise" where God's creatures no longer kill each other but feed together on grass, as a metaphor or figure of what life in God's coming Kingdom will be like. For when it is ushered in—

> They shall not hurt or destroy
>   in all my holy mountain;
> for the earth shall be full of the knowledge of the Lord
>   as the waters cover the sea.

(Isa. 11:9)

In his own less poetic way the author of Gen. 1 has a similar purpose in view. He is here for once quite plainly describing not the world as it is, but in a symbol the world as it ought to be. And he is, perhaps not so plainly, but unmistakably if we listen carefully, putting the blame on "man" for this state of affairs.

(iii)

And what of verse 31? "God saw everything that he had made, and behold, it was very good." It is good. But is it that good? Hardly. We have to recognize that from verse 26 in this chapter onwards—from the moment, that is, when "man" appears on the scene—irony and paradox are woven into its language. They do not cancel out the positive teaching of the story as a whole, that God created our world and everything in it and that his good providence overshadows it at all times. But like verse 2 with its picture of chaos, they remind us of the negative side. Evil is present in God's world—and now "man" is also present in it.

We are being subtly prepared for the story that comes next, when with a thump we are brought down from "man's" viceregal throne to his disobedience and his flouting of the Creator's will.

## THE SABBATH REST OF GOD

Genesis 2:1–4(a)

Thus the heavens and the earth were finished, and all the host of them. And on the seventh day God finished his work which he had done, and he rested on the seventh day from all his work which he had done. So God blessed the seventh day and hallowed it, because on it God rested from all his work which he had done in creation.

These are the generations of the heavens and the earth when they were created.

The seventh day is devoted to God's rest after his labours, after which in the first half of verse 4 there is a little summary referring to all that has gone before (the second half of that verse begins the next story of the Garden of Eden). The word "generations", which properly refers to the life story of a human being (as of Noah in 6:9), is metaphorically applied to the story of Creation, as though its two chief "characters" were the heavens and the earth and it an account of their family history.

### (i)

These verses describe God's retiral from the earthly scene, as he enters again upon the life of solitude he had given up six days previously in order to create the world. Needless to say, they do not mean that God ever literally abandoned his world, that even for a single day he withdrew the support of his providence, or that he ever would or ever could. The picture is part of the "fiction" of seven days around which the author structures his story, and it is to be interpreted imaginatively, not literally.

Just as the telescoping of the work of Creation into six days helped an unlettered people to take it all in, as it were, at one go, so God's resting on the seventh day brought it home to them that he need not have begun the work at all, that he could have chosen to live for all eternity with his own sufficient company, and that it was grace alone that moved him to make the heavens and the earth and people them with his creatures. It was a graphic way of teaching the lesson which more than any was dear to the author's own heart, that of God's transcendence, his holiness and apartness, his surpassing greatness and majesty, his utterly unique nature which we, his mere creatures, could only glimpse as he permitted us to glimpse it.

Milton catches beautifully the awe and splendour of the scene in a moving passage from *Paradise Lost:*

> The Planets in their stations list'ning stood,
> While the bright Pomp ascended jubilant.
> Open, ye everlasting gates, they sung,
> Open, ye heavens, your living doors; let in
> The great Creator from his work return'd
> Magnificent, his six days' work, a world.

(ii)

God blessed and hallowed this day. I am not going to raise here any controversy about the keeping of the Sabbath, except to say that the arguments advanced on both sides are far too often unworthy of these verses. The Church in its wisdom has combined the Jewish Sabbath with the celebration of Our Lord's Resurrection from the dead, and has filled the first day of the week with a rich and enduring symbolism. But the symbolism is infinitely more important than splitting hairs about what is and what is not permissible on it. And the symbolism is there even if the Church had not instituted such a day.

Human beings need rest (the Hebrew word *shabbat* means literally "cessation") from their toil, and no society can be healthy which does not recognize that need. But we also need rest from our care, from this life of getting and spending and laying waste our powers, which only faith in God can give us. In this faith we can find here the rest for our souls that Jesus promised (Matt. 11:28–30) and look forward hereafter to that sabbath rest which remains for the people of God (Heb. 4:9).

(iii)

But the chief association of the Sabbath, both in Judaism and in Christianity, is with worship. The story of Creation, then, ends fittingly with a strong reminder that we are in this world to praise and magnify God, and that only in so doing can we and all his creatures repay our debt to him who made us and by whose grace we survive.

I spoke earlier about the breath-taking symmetry of this story and how it reflects its author's understanding of the universe as a harmonious whole, designed by God in its every particular and governed at every moment by his sustaining providence. But there is another way in which the structure of the story can be displayed:

Darkness and Chaos

I
Light

| II<br>Firmament of heaven | | III<br>Earth |
|---|---|---|

IV
Lights

| V<br>Creatures of heaven | | VI<br>Creatures of earth |
|---|---|---|

VII
Rest

Arranged thus, the story takes on the contours of a temple building. As we enter its light from the darkness of chaos outside we are shown the whole of Creation arranged in order facing the Holy of Holies, behind which the Creator himself is concealed, and offering up to him the adoration and praise that is his due. And we are invited to share in their joyful worship.

Praise the Lord!
Praise the Lord from the heavens,
  praise him in the heights!
Praise him, all his angels,
  praise him, all his host!
Praise him, sun and moon,
  praise him, all you shining stars!
Praise him, you highest heavens,
  and you waters above the heavens!

Let them praise the name of the Lord!
  For he commanded and they were created.
And he established them for ever and ever;
  he fixed their bounds which cannot be passed.

Praise the Lord from the earth,
  you sea monsters and all deeps,
fire and hail, snow and frost,
  stormy wind fulfilling his command!
Mountains and all hills,
  fruit trees and all cedars!

Beasts and all cattle,
  creeping things and flying birds!
Kings of the earth and all peoples,
  princes and all rulers of the earth!
Young men and maidens together,
  old men and children!

Let them praise the name of the Lord,
  for his name alone is exalted;
  his glory is above earth and heaven.

(Ps. 148:1–13)

## THE STORY OF THE GARDEN OF EDEN

Genesis 2:4(b)–3:24

The story of Adam and Eve in the Garden of Eden begins halfway through verse 4 of Genesis Chapter 2 and continues to the end of Chapter 3. It is a story with a vital message for us

about God and our relationship to him. But before we concern
ourselves with that message, let us first read it over as a story,
noting simply at this stage how different it is in flavour and
presentation from the story of Creation which precedes it.
(Readers are invited at this point to go over these two chapters
carefully in their own Bibles.)


## ON STYLE IN GENESIS CHAPTERS TWO AND THREE

Genesis 2:4(b)–3:24 (*cont'd*)

I want in this and the following section to ask some questions
about style and structure similar to the ones we asked earlier in
the case of Chapter 1. I hope once again to be able to show that
far from being irrelevant to the message of the story, the
answers we give to these questions can quite crucially affect our
understanding of it. In this section I concentrate on matters of
style, the way the author writes his story.

(i)

The first thing that has to be said is that we are now dealing with
a different author from the priest who composed Chapter 1.

Chapters 2 and 3 are assigned by the scholars to the docu-
mentary source which they label "J". The "J" stands for the
divine name translated in English "The Lord", but which is in
Hebrew *Jahweh* or, as it is nowadays more commonly spelt,
*Yahweh,* the personal name of the God of Israel. In a strict
historical sense this name was not known to the Hebrews before
Moses' time (see Exod. 3:13–14), but this document habitually
uses it from the beginning. The other documents, more fastidi-
ous, restrict themselves in Genesis to the generic *Elohim* "God"
(like the "P" document in Chapter 1) or some other divine title.
In Gen. 2 and 3, as it happens, we have "The Lord God" in
narrative and "God" on its own in conversation (see 3:1–5), but
since in Genesis it is the use of *Yahweh* not *Elohim* that is odd,
only its presence is significant for authorship.

But we scarcely need the evidence of the divine names to tell us that the authors of Gen. 1 and of Gen. 2 and 3 are not the same. The quite different styles of the two stories, which can be sensed even in English translation, ought to make this plain to us. I am sure that if they were not a part of a Bible or "holy" book but could be judged freshly and without bias, most of us would readily recognize this.

(ii)

In Chapter 1 we had a very carefully worded narrative. It was, as we saw, straightforward enough in most of its language, and it made clever use of several well tried story-telling techniques. The most notable of these were the patterned repetitions and the foreshortening (by means of the "fiction" of six days) of a long process into a short one. Through such devices the author simplified things for his unlettered audience, enabling them to take in all the details of what happened in Creation unhurriedly, and yet at the same time to see them as part of a consistently planned whole.

Alongside these "popular" touches, however, we found now and again quite sophisticated terminology which betrayed his desire as a priest to avoid unseemly modes of expression, particularly when he was describing God's activity. Thus, though he knew that the people he was speaking to were familiar with Leviathan and Rahab, he refused to bring a chaos monster into his account. The thought of God doing battle with a dragon was too much for him to stomach. His use of the plural "us" of God and his ironical use of the word "image" of "man" pointed in the same direction. He was intent wherever he could on distancing the Creator from his creatures so that there might be no danger of him being brought down to their level.

In a sense, therefore, it could be said that as a writer he fell between two stools. He wanted to produce a good story that would hold the attention of ordinary folks, but he also wanted to be academically correct, even at the risk of pitching his account above their heads. I have the feeling that he may have caused as much perplexity as pleasure among his audience.

(iii)

The author of Gen. 2 and 3 clearly had no such inhibitions. Even a cursory glance through his story reveals him almost luxuriating in the very things which the author of Gen. 1 found so objectionable. His God is not the remote Creator-architect of Gen. 1, but as human and earthy as he can make him. At the start he is pictured as a potter fashioning "man" with his hands out of mud. But for most of the time he figures—and on the whole figures realistically—as merely one character among others, playing the role of the owner of a garden, who takes on Adam as his gardener and just like any human employer visits him from time to time to see how he is getting on. And that is not all. Gen. 1 would have nothing to do with a dragon, but in this story we have as bold as brass a snake that talks, and we have magical trees and fiercely armed angels (Cherubim) to boot. How naive and primitive it all sounds after the dignity and sobriety of Chapter 1!

It would, however, be a fatal mistake for us to conclude from this that the author of Gen. 2 and 3 was naive or primitive in his thinking. As we shall soon see, he was anything but. It was simply that he had a different idea from the author of Gen. 1 about how to go about his job as a story-teller.

Both authors were trying to say something to ordinary Hebrews about God's purpose in creating the world and its inhabitants, and this meant, living in the age they did, that they had to put their teaching into the form of a story. Both in the end perform their tasks with a great deal of skill. But whereas the author of Gen. 1 felt it necessary to touch up his story in the interests of theological propriety, the author of the Garden of Eden story seems to have done little more than mould more artistically the traditions available to him. He has intentionally preserved all the fantasy and extravagance of the kind of stories he knew his audience were used to, because in his judgment that was the way he could most effectively lead them on to appreciate the message he wished to get across. I suspect that most Hebrews would applaud that judgment, and that as a story they liked this better than the one which now precedes it in the Bible.

## ON STRUCTURE IN GENESIS CHAPTERS TWO AND THREE

### Genesis 2:4(b)–3:24 (*cont'd*)

When we were discussing the structure of Chapter 1 I made the point that many of the stories we nowadays regard as only fit for our children were, in less sophisticated times, enjoyed by adults as well. Like the stories of Genesis they began their lives in societies where people could not yet read and write but had to depend for their entertainment—and for much of their education as well—on the professional "singers of tales". It is not therefore so surprising as it might seem that folk stories the world over should turn out to be remarkably like each other.

I compared Gen. 1's structure of successive panels all built on the same pattern with the structure of "Chicken Licken", not itself an old story though in this respect using an old device. In this section I propose to attempt a similar exercise in the case of Gen. 2 and 3. But this time the "children's" story chosen for comparison—the story of Cinderella—is an ancient story, whose origin is lost in the mists of mediaeval Europe.

(i)

We can best analyse the structure or plot of this well-known tale in terms of a problem to be solved and of the various moves, at first unsuccessful but finally successful, by which the solution was arrived at. The problem is essentially how the heroine who has fallen into dire straits may be restored to happiness and prosperity.

The *first* move is the girl's attempt to alleviate her situation by trying to please her wicked stepmother and her two daughters, but this only makes them treat her more cruelly still. The *second* move is the invitation to the ball given by the King's son, which Cinderella, though by birth as eligible as her sisters, is not allowed to accept. The *third* move brings in the fairy godmother, with whose magical help, involving a pumpkin and some rats who turn into a coach and coachmen (this story's equivalent of Genesis' magic trees and talking snake?), Cinderella does in fact get to the ball. But this move is accompanied by a condition ("be back by midnight"), which Cinderella does not quite manage to keep, and in her failure she leaves her slipper behind. The *fourth* and eventually successful move is the prince's search for the owner of the slipper. Cinderella marries her prince and achieves the happiness she deserves.

We can perhaps see a *fifth* and final move in the generous way Cinderella forgives her sisters and finds husbands for them too. This restores the family unity which had been fragmented when Cinderella's natural mother died and her father remarried, and so fully solves the problem with which the story had begun.

(ii)

The story of the Garden of Eden is rather more complicated than that of Cinderella, and is almost two separate little stories run together, one (Chapter 2) in which there is a need to be met and the other (Chapter 3) in which, as in the fairy tale, there is a problem to be solved. But in each of these two parts (we may call them "Acts") a number of moves can be distinguished leading up respectively to the meeting of the need and the solving of the problem. And there is a link between the parts. It is supplied by the condition which God (acting almost like Cinderella's fairy godmother!) lays down. It is the failure of the hero and heroine to keep this condition, laid down in Chapter 2, which becomes the problem to be solved in Chapter 3.

Here is my suggested outline:

ACT I OR PARADISE

*The Need* (2:4(b)–7). God creates "man" as a "living being". The implication of this is that "man" cannot exist on his own.
*Move 1* (2:8–15). The man needs somewhere to live and work, so God creates for him the garden with its trees of immortality and knowledge.
*The Condition* (2:16–17). The man, however, is forbidden to eat from the tree of knowledge.

*Move 2* (2:18–20). The man needs a helpmeet, so God creates the animals to be subject to him and serve him.

*Move 3* (2:21–22). The animals do not meet this need, so God creates woman.

*The Need Met* (2:23–25). The man and the woman live together in the garden in harmony and innocence.

ACT II OR PARADISE LOST

*The Problem* (3:1–7). The man and the woman fail to keep the condition for living in Paradise. On the prompting of the serpent they eat of the forbidden fruit and gain knowledge. God must move to prevent this threat to his divinity, for what if they should now avail themselves of the fruit of immortality as well?

*Move 1* (3:8–13). God confronts the participants. They by their excuses and their accusations of each other show that the harmony of Paradise is irrevocably disrupted and its innocence irretrievably lost.

*Move 2* (3:14–19). God pronounces on each in turn punishments which draw attention to the enmity, suffering, toil, and eventually death which are the inevitable results of knowledge.

*Mitigation* (3:20–21). Nevertheless, the man and the woman will have children, and God will provide for their needs.

*Move 3* (3:22–23). God removes them from the garden to the world outside where, now mitigated but still severe, the sentences can take effect.

*The Problem Solved* (3:24). "Man" is banished from Paradise and no longer has access to immortality.

## ON HOW TO INTERPRET GENESIS CHAPTERS TWO AND THREE

### Genesis 2:4(b)–3:24 (*cont'd*)

I have said enough in the last two sections to show that in its style and its structure the story of the Garden of Eden is a typical piece of folk literature, and rather more a story of the common people than the story of Creation in Gen. 1. But how does this bear on our interpretation of it? Here also I believe that the story of Cinderella can help us.

(i)

It must be obvious that the people for whom it was first intended—and remember they were adults, not children—could have had no conceivable interest in whether a girl of that name ever existed. Indeed, the story itself, by creating a "never never" setting in which, unlike the real world where they lived, extraordinary and miraculous things were at any moment likely to happen, actively discouraged them from speculation of that kind.

Yet there was meaning in it for them. Possibly it encouraged them to think that if they behaved as faithfully and graciously as little Cinderella did, prosperity would come their way too. At the least it gave them a hope to hold onto amid the tedium and hardship of their everyday lives. In their more realistic moments they would know that the prospects of such a miracle happening to them were dim, but who was to prevent them having dreams? In its rather sentimental "from rags to riches" way the story of Cinderella is a genuine enough parable of the human situation in the dismal society which gave rise to it—and in not a few dismal societies since. We in this modern age, when as a rule only children read the story, may not immediately perceive this, but once it is pointed out to us, we are quite ready to accept it. It makes sense.

(ii)

It is my contention that if we approach the story of the Garden of Eden in a similarly imaginative spirit, everything will similarly fall into place.

The naive pictures of God as potter and landowner, the trees whose magical fruit conferred wonderful gifts, the talking snake, the guardian Cherubim, the very garden itself—all these are but the furniture of the story. They are not part of its underlying meaning. There never was such a place as the Garden of Eden, nor was there ever a historical person called Adam who lived in it and conversed with snakes and with God in Hebrew. The garden is a garden of the mind, a garden of "men's" dreams, the kind of place they would like this world to be, the kind of place indeed they know this world ought to be. And Adam is each one of us, he is "Everyman". That this world is not what it should be is due to "man's" disobedience of God, to the sinful Adam in us all. Each and every day Paradise beckons us, but each and every day we eat the forbidden fruit and are banished from it.

Interpreted like this, the story of the Garden of Eden also becomes a parable of the human situation, but at a much more profound level than any fairy tale could aspire to. Both it and the story of Cinderella paint for us a symbolic picture of the mocking contrast that exists between "man's" potential and his actual state. But whereas the fairy tale runs out in sentimentality and romance, the Biblical story remorselessly brings "man" face to face with his authentic self, and it lays the blame for the contrast not on misfortune or fate but squarely on his own shoulders. It begins with enchantment, but ends by confronting him with the reality of what the Bible calls sin.

### (iii)

In this short summary I have uncovered only a fraction of the rich symbolism that lurks beneath the surface of Gen. 2 and 3. We will need to put a lot more work into these chapters before we can claim (if we ever can claim) to have plumbed all its depths. But perhaps I may claim to have pointed the way. We must not expect a story of this kind to yield historical or scientific information. If this supercilious generation wishes to get anything out of it, they must become as little children again and see it with the eyes of ancient wonder and of ancient wisdom.

### "MAN'S" DEPENDENCE ON GOD

Genesis 2:4(b)-7

In the day that the Lord God made the earth and the heavens, when no plant of the field was yet in the earth and no herb of the field had yet sprung up—for the Lord God had not caused it to rain upon the earth, and there was no man to till the ground; but a mist went up from the earth and watered the whole face of the ground—then the Lord God formed man of dust from the ground, and breathed into his nostrils the breath of life; and man became a living being.

These introductory verses supply the wider setting of the story and introduce the two chief characters, God and "man".

(i)

It has been claimed that we have here an alternative account of Creation to that in Chapter 1. There is some truth in this in so far as the order in which the plants which are mentioned and "man" are created is the reverse of Chapter 1's order. There "man" comes last, three days after the earth's vegetation, whereas here it is explicitly stated that there were no "plants" or "herbs" in existence when he was created.

However, I don't think that the author of Gen. 2 and 3 is at all interested in the sequence of Creation. The things he mentions are mentioned only because they are relevant to the outcome of his story. There were no "plants of the field" and no wild shrubs or bushes (this is a better translation than "herbs") for the simple reason that both of these are associated in the story with the curse on the ground in 3:18. The plants of the field are therefore the crops of grain which after his expulsion from the garden "man" will have to produce with the sweat of his brow, and the shrubs or bushes are the thorns and thistles which will then grow up among them.

The rain and "mist" of these verses are to be similarly explained. Wild shrubs like thorns and thistles required rain, so naturally it cannot yet have fallen. On the other hand, there had to be underground water, because there were shortly to be trees and rivers in Eden. It is probably to this underground water that the difficult word translated "mist" or (in the RSV footnote) "flood" refers.

The wider setting of the story is therefore the earth as the author imagines it to have been before, as a result of "man's" sin, it became the earth as it is now.

(ii)

There follows in verse 7 the rather crude statement that God put "man" together out of bits of dust and breathed breath into him so that almost like a little Pinocchio he came alive.

The word translated "being" in the RSV is in Hebrew *nephesh*. The AV has "soul", which the RSV wisely avoids because it might have made its modern readers think about the "immortality" of the soul. This is not a Hebrew but a Greek idea. In Hebrew the "soul" is not a part of "man" but the whole living person, consisting, as this verse makes clear, of his body plus the breath which gives it life. When the Psalmist says "God will ransom my soul from the power of Sheol" (Ps. 49:15), he is not therefore to be understood as looking forward to the survival of his soul after death. He is simply expressing his confidence that God will not let him die. And when he says "Bless the Lord, O my soul" (Ps. 103:1, 2, 22; Ps. 104:1, 35), he means simply that he wants to sing to God with his whole being (compare Ps. 104:33).

The naivety of this picture of God forming "man" like a potter should not be allowed to blind us to its essential meaning. This is that we and all human beings derive our lives directly from him. Without the breath that he puts into us we are dead and our bodies dissolve into the dust from which they came. As Ecclesiastes says (12:7), "the dust returns to the earth as it was, and the spirit (or better, breath) returns to God who gave it." Or as the author of this story later has God saying, "you are dust, and to dust you shall return" (3:19). These quotations show that the origin of every human being could to the Hebrews be described in the same pictorial language.

This lesson of "man's" utter creatureliness is even more starkly present in the Hebrew of this verse than it is in English. For the Hebrew word for "man" is *adam* and the Hebrew word for "ground" is *adamah*. The two words have no etymological connection with each other, but they were so close in sound that the author could not resist the play. Nor could he in the verses that follow resist rubbing in the lesson wherever he could by constantly using the word "ground". We have it throughout this story—see 2:9, 19; 3:17, 19, 23—and we have it throughout the next story of Cain and Abel for which he was also responsible—see 4:2, 3, 10–12, 14.

How different all this is from the Greek view that a person's material body may perish but that his or her "soul" will live for ever! That view only became familiar to Judaism and Christianity when in later centuries they moved into the Greek-speaking world, and it has caused untold theological damage ever since. In Hebrew thinking there is nothing of eternal worth in human beings as such and they can only come into contact with eternity when they relate themselves humbly and in obedience to God their Creator (see further the commentary on 1:26–31, *"Man"—the creature of God*).

Can we have any doubt which view is the more realistic?

### (iii)

"Man" cannot even begin to live without God. If there is anything else implied in these introductory verses it is that he cannot live either without the animals or without others of his own kind, nor indeed without a job of work to do. These things also belong to the teaching of the Bible about "man", and they are so clearly brought out in this chapter that the meeting of his needs for a social environment and companionship has become the main plot-motif in the first half of the story. "Man" cannot live on his own. But for the moment it is his dependence on God that is stressed.

## THE GARDEN OF DELIGHT

Genesis 2:8–15

> And the Lord God planted a garden in Eden, in the east; and there he put the man whom he had formed. And out of the ground the Lord God made to grow every tree that is pleasant to the sight and good for food, the tree of life also in the midst of the garden, and the tree of the knowledge of good and evil.
>
> A river flowed out of Eden to water the garden, and there it divided and became four rivers. The name of the first is Pishon; it is

the one which flows around the whole land of Havilah, where there is gold; and the gold of that land is good; bdellium and onyx stone are there. The name of the second river is Gihon; it is the one which flows around the whole land of Cush. And the name of the third river is Tigris, which flows east of Assyria. And the fourth river is the Euphrates.

The Lord God took the man and put him in the garden of Eden to till it and keep it.

In these verses we have a description of the more immediate stage on which the action of the story is played out, the Garden of Eden and its trees and rivers. In terms of the plot the garden is God's answer to the man's need for an environment in which to live and work.

(i)

There are several other references in the Old Testament to the Garden of Eden or, as it is sometimes called, the Garden of God. In Gen. 13:10 the land chosen by Lot is described as well-watered like the Garden of the Lord. In Joel 2:3 the prophet warns the people that the land on which they dwell will in retrospect seem a Garden of Eden when the Day of the Lord comes and it is turned into a desolate wilderness. In Isa. 51:3 the exiles in Babylon are comforted by the thought that on their return to Zion, God will make her wilderness like Eden and her desert like the Garden of the Lord.

None of these references seems to be alluding explicitly to this story but to be using the names loosely as figures of somewhere desirable to live, much as we ourselves might use the phrase "enchanted island" or indeed the words "Paradise" or "heaven". As befits an eastern environment the chief point of the comparison is of water over against dryness, of an oasis over against the unending desert.

(ii)

A couple of longer passages in Ezekiel Chapters 28 and 31 are a bit more forthcoming with details.

The first of these is a tirade against the king of Tyre for behaving as though he were a god when he was but a man (28:9). The prophet, addressing him in the true God's name, says:

> You were in Eden, the garden of God;
> every precious stone was your covering ...
> With an anointed guardian cherub I placed you;
> you were on the holy mountain of God (verses 13 and 14).

But now that his heart had become proud, God had cast him down from the mountain and the guardian Cherub had driven him out from the midst of the precious stones (verse 16), and he would soon come to a dreadful end (verse 19).

The oracle in Chapter 31 is directed against the Egyptian Pharaoh and compares him to a lofty cedar in Lebanon. It goes on:

> The cedars in the garden of God
> could not rival it ...
> and all the trees of Eden envied it (verses 8 and 9).

But this cedar "set its top among the clouds" (verse 10). Therefore the most terrible of nations would come to cut it down (verse 12).

Again there does not seem to be any direct connection with the Genesis story, though in these passages there are references not only to trees and precious stones (as in the present passage) and to a guardian Cherub (compare Gen. 3:24), but to someone being thrown out of the garden. We are probably in touch not with Gen. 2 and 3, but with a pagan story about the home of the gods, the beautiful place far away which they inhabited, and about how once upon a time a rebellious angel was cast out of it for daring to challenge the father of the gods.

This story, though not a Hebrew story, must have been well known in Israel. For not only did the name Eden (meaning "delight" or "pleasantness" or "luxury") become in Hebrew a synonym for the ideal place which men and women dream about, but a prophet like Ezekiel could compare the king of Tyre to the deity who was cast out of it and the Pharaoh to one of its splendid trees, and be immediately understood. It is not surprising, therefore, that the author of Gen. 2 and 3 decided to use it as the starting point of a quite different kind of story, in which the garden is inhabited not by the gods but by the first "man", and it is not a rebellious god nor a proud human tyrant but sinful humanity who are expelled from it.

(*Note:* It is possible that the same or a similar pagan story lies behind the later Jewish and Christian idea of Satan as a rebellious angel thrown down from heaven, but that is another development in another age.)

(iii)

Here the garden is located in the East and a river flows through it which on leaving it splits into four. Two of these rivers are the familiar Tigris and Euphrates in Mesopotamia, but we should not make too much of this and conclude that an actual historical place is intended. The identity of the other two rivers, Pishon and Gihon, and the lands associated with them, Havilah and Cush, has been endlessly debated, not only by modern scholars but by the Rabbis and Christian Fathers of earlier times, and with no agreement among them. It may well be that they are for the author fictional places like the land of Nod to which Cain flees (Gen. 4:16), which was also in the mysterious East.

The descriptions, half real, half imaginary, will then be meant to conjure up a picture of a country in, but not quite of, the known world, a country which we would all like to reach but which is always just out of reach over the next range of mountains or beyond the horizon. And this is, I think, exactly the impression the author wishes to leave with us. Eden is a country where men and women ought to be, it is accessible to them, but for a reason which he is about to give, no human being has yet got to it.

## THE TREES OF LIFE AND KNOWLEDGE

Genesis 2:8–15 (*cont'd*)

Among the many marvellous trees of the garden are two

which are singled out by name as especially important, the tree
of life and the tree of the knowledge of good and evil. The very
fact that they are given these names shows that it is only the
surface story that is concerned with trees. The names are what
really matter and they have to do with the underlying meaning.

(i)

There are a number of parallels to the tree of life in the "myths"
of other peoples. From the ancient East there is the plant which
figures in the story of Utnapishtim, the Mesopotamian Noah,
which is contained in the famous Gilgamesh Epic. We will be
looking at this story later, but for just now it is enough to note
that Utnapishtim received the plant after he survived the Flood,
and that he gives it to Gilgamesh to enable him to regain his
youth. However, while Gilgamesh is carrying it off, it is stolen
from him. So, it is implied, is eternal youth lost to humankind.

There is also the story of Adapa, who is summoned to visit
the gods but is warned by a goddess not to take the food and
water of life when offered them by the king of the gods, for they
were really death. Believing the lie, the hero is deprived of
immortality—and so, it is implied, by the will of the gods are all
human beings.

These pagan stories reflect the age-old agony of "men"
when faced with death and their perplexity that all that is good
and worthwhile in life should come to so abrupt an end. All too
often it has seemed to them as though the very gods were
conspiring to deprive them of what they might have had.

There is no mention of a tree of life in the Ezekiel passages we
referred to earlier, so we have no means of knowing whether
allusions like Prov. 3:18 and 15:4 comparing now wisdom and
now a gentle tongue to a "tree of life" go back to the story he
uses or to the story which is reproduced here. But the allusions
at least show that the idea was, like that of the Garden of Eden,
familiar enough to ordinary Hebrews and that they like other
ancient peoples were not averse to speculating about the
enigma of death.

(ii)

However, the author of Gen. 2 and 3 is obviously much more interested in another problem, the problem of knowledge. The tree of life plays a secondary role compared with the second named tree, the tree of the knowledge of good and evil. It is not the prospect of death but the possession of knowledge that constitutes for his story the cutting edge of the human situation.

There are again parallels elsewhere, if not exactly to a tree of knowledge, at least to knowledge as a theme, but they are not so close as those to the tree of life. In the Adapa story just mentioned the hero is given wisdom but fails to gain immortality. This would be not unlike what happens in Genesis if it were not plain that immortality was the story's main theme and that wisdom is regarded as a good thing for "man" to have.

There is also the more modern story of Faust, who sells his soul to the Devil in exchange for knowledge and has to pay the price in Hell. Here we do have a more negative view taken of knowledge or at any rate of its consequences. As Marlowe puts it in his play:

> Hell hath no limits nor is circumscrib'd
> In one self place: where we are is Hell,
> And where Hell is, there must we ever be.

(*Doctor Faustus*)

But we do not get in the story of Faust the very perturbing idea that we get in this story that the acquiring of knowledge is itself the chief ingredient of human sin. This, it seems, is a uniquely Hebrew idea.

(iii)

What then is this knowledge of good and evil which according to this story is not to be found in Paradise but only in Paradise Lost? If we put it that way it becomes clear that it cannot be merely moral discrimination, the ability to know what is right and what is wrong. Nor can it be simply the ability to distinguish between what is beneficial and useful and what is harmful and dangerous. How could God possibly wish the knowledge of such things to be denied to "man"?

We can only understand what the author is getting at in this piece of symbolism by tying in the symbolism with his story. In the story we are told *two* things about what happened when the man and the woman ate the fruit of the forbidden tree:

(a) As the serpent forecast (3:5) and as God himself admitted later (3:22), they became like God (or, as we could translate, like the angels), knowing good and evil.

(b) Where before they had been naked and were not ashamed (2:25), they now knew that they were naked and quickly covered themselves (3:7).

It is not therefore simply a generalized "knowledge" that lies at the root of "man's" fall from grace but two specific aspects or, if you like, results of knowledge.

The first of these is easier to grasp than the second, since we have a passage in 2 Sam. 14:17 which gives us the guidance we need. In this passage the wise woman of Tekoa praises Absalom for having wisdom "like the angel of God to discern good and evil". A little later (verse 20) she says, obviously meaning the same thing, that he has wisdom "like the angel of God to know all things that are on earth". The phrase "good and evil" could, it seems, mean in Hebrew something like our phrase "good, bad, and indifferent". It was a colourful way of saying "everything".

It is therefore the kind of knowledge that belongs to divinity, to the angels and thus ultimately only to God himself, that is forbidden to humanity, the kind of full and comprehensive knowledge that brings to its owner power and independence. "Men" are being told that they must not set their sights on a divine status that cannot be their's, but should remember their creatureliness and their dependence upon God for everything they have. And they are being told that they are setting their sights on divinity when they aspire to know everything.

This is a hard message for our modern age when "man's" insatiable search for knowledge is almost universally commended. We are in the habit of arguing that the possession of knowledge should be distinguished from the use to which people put it. The author of Gen. 2 and 3 does not make any such distinction, and would regard it as evading the issue. To him knowledge and sin are inextricably bound up together. We don't get anything like this in the stories of Israel's neighbours. The tree of knowledge is a characteristically Hebrew tree, unparalleled in antiquity and, it would seem, also hitting today's favourite philosophies where they think themselves strongest.

At this point I would like to leave the subject of the tree of knowledge for the time being. I have still to comment on the other line of thought about the man and the woman being naked and full of shame after eating its fruit. But that is better postponed till we reach the part of the story (at 3:7) where it comes most into prominence.

### "MAN'S" TASK IN THE GARDEN

Genesis 2:8–15 (*cont'd*)

Into this ideal environment God introduces the man whom he had made and entrusts him with the job of "tilling" the garden and "keeping" it (verse 15). I wish only to make a couple of short comments on this verse, but symbolically they are very important ones.

(i)

The first verb "till" shrewdly reminds us that Paradise and work are not incompatible, and that ideas of Paradise as a place where as if by magic all we need falls from the trees and we can sit back in idleness and enjoy it, are not Hebrew ideas. In the Biblical Paradise "man" is required to work. God has so made us that we cannot be truly human unless we have a job of work to do. And he has so made the earth that it can only become a Paradise when "man's" work is mixed with its bounty and beauty.

(ii)

This meaning of "tending" is also involved in the second verb, which is translated by the NEB "care for". But it has an additional, indeed more common, nuance which that rendering does not catch. The Hebrew verb means also "to guard", and is in fact the same verb as is used in 3:24 of the Cherubim "guarding" the way to the tree of life. Symbolically this means that "man" has a God-given duty not only to cultivate but to *protect* the earth if it is ever to become an Eden where he and God may converse together. It is not his to exploit for his own ends. The picture is naively simple, but we are not far from the concept of "man's" stewardship over nature so splendidly set forth in the previous chapter (see commentary on 1:26-31, *"Man"—the viceroy of God*).

Rather than translate "guard" here, however, I would retain the older rendering "keep", which is in touch with both senses of the verb. With the AV we should use it at 3:24 as well. This would enable English readers to share in a very nice irony that is present in the original Hebrew. The keeper of the trees himself does what in the story it was part of his duty to prevent, eats from the only one that must not be eaten, and so has to be replaced!

## GOD'S CONDITION FOR LIFE IN PARADISE

Genesis 2:16-17

> And the Lord God commanded the man, saying, "You may freely eat of every tree of the garden; but of the tree of the knowledge of good and evil you shall not eat, for in the day that you eat of it you shall die."

In the plot of the story these verses contain what may be called the contract of employment which God as the owner of the garden hands to the man as he takes over his task of tending and guarding it. His remuneration is the fruit with which the garden abounds, but there is one tree in the middle of it from which he is told he must not eat on pain of death. A condition is placed upon his freedom of action.

(i)

On a plain reading of the text it is difficult to avoid the conclusion that at this point God is guilty of telling a lie. The man breaks the condition, but he is not instantly put to death as God threatened.

Our immediate reaction to this is one of shock. Surely it cannot be so. So we begin to probe, and before long we come up with what seems to be a satisfactory explanation. Although the man may not immediately have died on eating the forbidden tree, he did become subject to death and eventually he did die. God's warning that "on the day" he ate the fruit he would "surely die" (the RSV ought not to have omitted the "surely" of the AV, which is there in the Hebrew) was not therefore a lie, but a rather stern way of drawing the man's attention to the ultimate consequence of his disobedience. It should perhaps be translated, "From the very day that you eat of it you are doomed to die."

But this line of argument will not do. God's statement may not be a downright lie like the "whopper" the goddess told Adapa in the Mesopotamian story mentioned a few pages ago, but it is not straight talking either. We are not taking the man's position at the time into account. He must obviously have understood it as a threat of instant death, otherwise it could have held no terrors for him. Furthermore, God does not tell the man the whole truth. He says nothing of the more attractive consequences of disobedience. It is left to the serpent to tempt him with the prospect of becoming like "the angels" and achieving the independence that knowledge brings.

We may wriggle out of the difficulty in verse 17 by rendering it more freely than the Hebrew strictly permits. It is an enigmatic statement and it can at a stretch be taken two ways. But we cannot excise from the story as a whole the impression that God acts in an underhand manner.

When all allowances that can be made are made, we have to

admit that there is not in the end all that much difference between God's behaviour here and that of the goddess in the Adapa story. But perhaps that similarity gives us the necessary clue to explain the incident. It reminds us once again that the author is not writing a theological treatise but trying to compose a compelling story which will make his audience sit up and take notice.

As I see it, the main point of God's deceit is not at all to suggest that God normally behaves like that, though this notion would not have perturbed a Hebrew audience nearly so much as it perturbs us. It is to underline God's total abhorrence of "man's" proneness to disobey. So much did he hate sin that he was prepared to go to any lengths to prevent it. By picturing God as having to indulge in deceit, the author is inviting us in our imaginations to look into the Father's heart and see the turmoil that at this most crucial of all moments was there.

A much more enlightening parallel than the pagan story of Adapa is the parable of the Importunate Widow in Luke 18:1–8, which is one of Our Lord's most daring. There Jesus compares God to a disgruntled judge who gives justice to a poor woman not because it is her due but because she pesters him so long and loud that he is willing to do anything to be quit of her. We don't need to be told that Jesus is not encouraging us to think of God as unfeeling or unfair. We don't even need the Evangelist's comment in verse 1 about not losing heart in prayer. We let our imaginations guide us and once having got the point, we stop.

In the same way we ought to let our imaginations guide us through this more ancient parable. Its word-pictures both of God and of "man" are not to be pressed further than the story demands.

(ii)

Let us turn now to the deeper meaning of this passage. At that level it is of course no longer speaking of something that happened long ago, but addressing life in the present. It shows us "man" confronted with a choice: "You may freely eat . . .",

"You shall not eat . . ." "Man" can either work for God and find happiness and freedom in serving him, or he can go his own way thinking he knows all there is to know, and live with the inevitable consequences. This is the most fundamental choice that any of us is ever called upon to face, the choice between God and ourselves, between real freedom and the illusion of it, between Paradise and Hell, between life and death. It is our choice and our choice only. God cannot interfere, otherwise it is not a genuine choice. But how anxious he is that we make the right choice, how devastated when we make the wrong one!

(iii)

There is one further point worth making. The prohibition does not mention the other tree in the garden, the tree of life. We are simply told about it at the beginning, after which it drops out of sight till the end of the story. But the implication of this passage is that is was not forbidden to the man. What a beautifully ironic comment this is on human nature! All the time the man and woman were in the garden they had the chance of immortality but did not avail themselves of it, no doubt because their minds were so set on what they had been told they could not have. So near and yet so far!

## ONE WITH NATURE

Genesis 2:18–25

Then the Lord God said, "It is not good that the man should be alone; I will make him a helper fit for him." So out of the ground the Lord God formed every beast of the field and every bird of the air, and brought them to the man to see what he would call them; and whatever the man called every living creature, that was its name. The man gave names to all cattle, and to the birds of the air, and to every beast of the field; but for the man there was not found a helper fit for him.

So the Lord God caused a deep sleep to fall upon the man, and while he slept took one of his ribs and closed up its place with flesh;

and the rib which the Lord God had taken from the man he made
into a woman and brought her to the man. Then the man said,

"This at last is bone of my bones
and flesh of my flesh;
she shall be called Woman,
because she was taken out of Man."

Therefore a man leaves his father and his mother and cleaves to his
wife, and they become one flesh. And the man and his wife were both
naked, and were not ashamed.

These verses introduce the third and fourth characters, one—
the woman—directly, the other—the serpent—indirectly, since
as we later find out, it is one of the animals now created by God.
In terms of the plot the animals (including the birds) and the
woman are brought into being to be companions to the man
and to alleviate his loneliness.

(i)

It is to be noted that the sequence of Creation is again different
from that in Chapter 1. In this story the order is man—the
animals—woman. There the birds were created (along with the
fish, not mentioned here) on the fifth day and the land animals
on the sixth day, and (also on the sixth day but after the
animals) man and woman were created in the self-same act. But
these outward differences apart (and they are outward unless
we are looking for scientific or historical truth in Genesis), the
inward lesson of each story is remarkably similar. All living
beings as creatures of the one Creator are bound together in a
unity which cannot be disrupted without doing violence to his
purposes for the world.

(ii)

In the case of Gen. 1 this lesson was emphasized by the phrase
"according to their kinds", which gave every bird and fish and
animal (and indeed every plant as well) its inalienable right to
existence and its unique place in God's scheme of things. "Man"
was assigned a position of authority over them, but the description of him as the "image" of God was not, as it has been so

often and so tragically understood, a *carte blanche* for him to exploit them as he saw fit. His authority was a delegated authority as God's viceroy. There was a strong implication that he would be required to give an account of his stewardship, and that he would not find this an easy thing to do.

In this passage the lesson is more endearingly put. We do not have to rack our brains to grasp what the author is getting at, but are shown a simple but exquisitely tender picture of God himself leading the animals to the man and waiting expectantly to see what he should call them. As in Gen. 1 (where it is God who gives the names) this act of naming symbolizes power over them. It was up to the man to decide what each should do. But the abrasive tones of Chapter 1's "have dominion" and "subdue" are missing, and in their place is tranquillity and trust and harmony. It is a great pity that in our dealings with our fellow creatures we have taken our cue from Gen. 1's harsh verbs far more often than we have modelled ourselves on this gentle scene.

## ONE FLESH

Genesis 2:18–25 (*cont'd*)

### (iii)

The scene which follows is equally elemental in its beauty and its appeal. God sends a deep sleep on the man and as he sleeps, removes one of his ribs and out of it makes a woman (the Hebrew says actually "built it up into"). Then like a father giving away his daughter at her wedding, he conducts her to the man, who cries out in joy, "This (is it) at last!" A "helper fit for him" has been found, as the RSV puts it in one of its less happy renderings. It should have retained the AV's "help meet for him", which has given the English language one of its loveliest words (how sad that it is usually and ignorantly corrupted into "helpmate"!). The man shouts joyfully because he recognizes another human being who can do for him what the animals could not, give him the companionship of his own kind and share with him his whole life. He gives her a name which identifies her as "one flesh" with himself, *ishshah* "woman" because she was taken from *ish* "man" (it is fortunate that English can reproduce the Hebrew pun here; many languages cannot), and naked and without shame they live together in the garden.

(iv)

It is almost a crime to lard so touching a scene with prosaic comment, but there are a number of things that can and must be said:

(a) The passage does not sanction man's precedence over woman but simply accepts it. The Bible knows nothing about equal rights for women in exactly the same way that it knows nothing about political democracy, because neither had been heard of at the time. It takes relationships as they were in that ancient world and without changing then outwardly transforms them inwardly. No Hebrew husband who took this passage to heart would lord it over his wife, and no Hebrew wife would go in fear of unjust treatment. For here is a more basic rule for life between the sexes (and for that matter, between human beings in general) than any legislation could ever devise—the rule of joy and partnership and innocence and love.

(b) At the same time it cannot be entirely irrelevant that the woman comes last. Robert Burns could write humorously with this passage in mind:

> Auld nature swears, the lovely dears
> Her noblest work she classes O;
> Her prentice han' she tried on man,
> An' then she made the lasses O.
> *(Green grow the Rashes)*

But he was saying more than he knew (or am I doing our Scottish bard an injustice?). The male virtues have got this world in a fearful mess, and it is high time that the female virtues were given a chance. Surely it was part of the author's intention to hint at this!

(c) Verse 24 should properly be in brackets. It is an aside of the story-teller, forgetting himself for once and stepping outside his tale. He must have had a strong reason for doing this. That he should speak of the man rather than the woman leaving the parental home shows that it had nothing to do with explaining or justifying some wedding custom. My own feeling is that he simply wanted to make sure that his audience had got the message. It is the "one flesh" that he wishes to underline. The union of man and woman is the closest relationship that human beings can experience, closer even than that between a father and mother and their children. It is the ideal symbol of the bond that ought to exist between all people the world over. God intended all humankind to be "one flesh".

(d) We damage the symbolism of this passage if we pay too much attention to the word "naked" and begin at this point, just when the author is putting the last brick of his picture of Paradise into place, to think about sex. That religious people down the centuries have done exactly that tells us more about their obsession with sex than it does about the author's intention. He is telling a parable about the whole of human life as it ought to be. I will be returning to the word "naked" when we reach the commentary on 3:7. Here I would only insist that the vital words are not "were naked" but "were not ashamed". It is not the sex life of Paradise (or the lack of it) that the story-teller is emphasizing but the garden's joyful innocence in every respect.

(v)

The vision of Paradise is at an end. At the risk of repeating myself I must warn the reader once more against interpreting it historically, otherwise he will have to take seriously all the "fairy tale" furniture with which it is crammed. Ancient peoples had apparently no difficulty with this kind of story, judging by the number of them that they passed down. They sensed intuitively what the point was. What we labour to describe as the potential and the actual of "man" they put into story form as the before and after. Thus in the first part of this old Hebrew story what human beings should be—at peace and in harmony with God, with each other, and with the world of nature—has become a Paradise in the remote past. What human beings are—the inhabitants not of Paradise but of Paradise Lost—is the theme of its second part.

It would be nice if we could stay with the man and the woman and the animals in the garden, and say with Milton:

> Sleep on,
> Blest pair; and O yet happiest if ye seek
> No happier state, and know to know no more.
>
> (*Paradise Lost*)

But we cannot. The real world outside calls us.

## THIS DARK WORLD OF SIN

Genesis 3:1-7

Now the serpent was more subtle than any other wild creature that the Lord God had made. He said to the woman, "Did God say, 'You shall not eat of any tree of the garden'?" And the woman said to the serpent, "We may eat of the fruit of the trees of the garden; but God said, 'You shall not eat of the fruit of the tree which is in the midst of the garden, neither shall you touch it, lest you die.'" But the serpent said to the woman, "You will not die. For God knows that when you eat of it your eyes will be opened, and you will be like God, knowing good and evil." So when the woman saw that the tree was good for food, and that it was a delight to the eyes, and that the tree was to be desired to make one wise, she took of its fruit and ate; and she also gave some to her husband, and he ate. Then the eyes of both were opened, and they knew that they were naked; and they sewed fig leaves together and made themselves aprons.

In the plot of the story Chapter 3 is a second "Act" telling how God moved to contain the consequences that followed when the man and the woman broke the condition imposed by him for life in his garden.

In order to get at the deeper meaning of the story, however, it is essential to turn the sequence of events on its head. At this level Chapter 3 describes not what happened in remote history to our first ancestor and his wife, but the situation in which all human beings find themselves at the present time. And they find themselves in that situation because they disobey God everyday, and so everyday see the gates to a fuller and more perfect life being slammed in their faces. In the real life of human beings Paradise does not precede disobedience but follows obedience. It is there beckoning them, and but for one thing God would welcome them into it with open arms. That one thing is what the Bible calls sin.

(i)

Where in all this does the serpent fit in? All we are told about him before he begins to speak is that he was more subtle than any other wild creature that the Lord God had made.

This is of course fantasy, but it is not—as we have surely learned by this time—to be denigrated because of that. Animals only speak in fables, but fables contain much wisdom. They are usually wry comments on the quirks and foibles of human nature. The foxes and wolves and lions and hens which inhabit them represent character types or traits that we can easily recognize in ourselves and in other people—cunning, rashness, boastfulness, gullibility, and so on. Here is a typical Jewish one from the mediaeval period, entitled "On the advantage of being a scholar". I have chosen it not only because it is funny-wise like many another fable, but because it is perhaps not all that far away in what it says from some of what this commentary has been saying (see particularly on 1:26–31, *I have given every green plant*).

A fox looked up into a tree and saw a crow sitting on the topmost branch. The crow looked mighty good to him, for he was hungry. He tried every wile to get him down, but the wise old crow only leered contemptuously down at him.

"Foolish crow!" the fox said, banteringly. "Believe me, you have no reason to be afraid of me. Don't you know that the birds and beasts will never have to fight again? Haven't you heard the Messiah is coming? If you were a Talmud scholar like me, you'd surely know that the Prophet Isaiah has said that when the Messiah comes, 'the lion shall lie down with the lamb and the fox with the crow, and there shall be peace forevermore.'"

And as he stood there speaking sweetly, the baying of hounds was heard. The fox began to tremble with fright.

"Foolish fox!" croaked the crow pleasantly from the tree. "You have no reason to be afraid, since you're a Talmud scholar and know what the Prophet Isaiah has said."

"True, *I* know what the Prophet Isaiah said," cried the fox as he slunk off into the bushes, "but the trouble is the dogs don't."

(cited from Ausubel's *Treasury of Jewish Folklore*)

We smile and nod when we hear such a fable. But why shouldn't the Hebrews of Biblical times have had their fables too, and smiled and nodded when the serpent came on the scene in this story? It is not that this story is a mere fable, but it is at this juncture making use of the techniques of a fable. A large number of fables are in fact temptation scenes not unlike the one it portrays. What goes on in the human heart is externalized and distributed among a number of characters, in a fable usually all animals, sometimes trees and flowers, in this scene a snake and a woman and a man. It is clear that one of the reasons the snake has been selected for the role it plays is that like the fox it is universally credited with cunning, and it was slimy and treacherous to boot.

(ii)

The scene is replete with psychological subtlety and innuendo.

As one of the animals named by the man in the previous chapter, the serpent is assumed to be conversant with what had gone on there. It does not approach "the boss" directly, however, but addresses the woman first, getting at him through his subordinate. It then overstates outrageously what God had said in his prohibition, suggesting to the woman that every single tree had been forbidden them. She rushes to God's defence. "He didn't say that. It's only the one tree in the middle of the garden that's out of bounds. If we eat or even touch its fruit we will die." But she too overstates what God said. She adds "neither shall you touch it", revealing immediately how the prohibition had been needling them, and handing the tempter an advantage.

The serpent's next statement shows it as much the "Talmud scholar" as the fox in the fable we have just quoted. Like the man and the woman it is aware of the name of the forbidden tree, but unlike them it sees what it really signifies. They would not die but would become as knowledgeable and resourceful as the angels (in view of "one of us" in verse 22 we should probably translate *Elohim* in verse 5 by "angels", or even "gods" as does the AV; see the commentary on 1:26–31, *Let us make* . . .). This reply is in fact more true than God's prohibition, if only the immediate future is in prospect. But is it not in accord with the tug of temptation to be concerned only with the satisfaction of the moment? At any rate, the woman is now hopelessly hooked.

She sees with fresh eyes how tasty-looking is the tree's fruit and how attractive it is to the sight. What a pleasant way to become wise! A whole gamut of emotions is displayed before us, from the coarsely sensual through the pleasingly aesthetic to the arrogantly intellectual. It is what 1 John 2:16 (with this passage in mind?) calls "the lust of the flesh and the lust of the eyes and the pride of life". The serpent must be right. The woman yields to temptation, eats the fruit, and carries some to her husband. In a flash he recognizes what she has done and in a flash approves (he cannot have been unsuspecting, for was he not the gardener?), and he eats too. In a flash they both realize what they have done, but it is too late. They find—and again this is what usually happens when one succumbs to temptation—that forbidden fruit is not so sweet after as before.

### (iii)

In this masterpiece of a scene sin is, almost without our noticing it, set forth for what it is. It is beside the point to assign individual blame to the characters. The serpent is temptation personified, and the woman and the man are sin personified, not the woman more than the man but the two of them together. For all of this goes on in the heart of each one of us.

Sin is then first of all disobedience of God. It is doing what we know he wants us not to do, and it is not doing what we know he wants us to do. And it is discontent. It is being dissatisfied with what he has given us. And it is self-deceit. It is longing for an illusory freedom when we can only be free as we obey him. And it is pride. It is thinking that we can run our affairs better than he can. Above all it is rebellion. It is usurping God's role and chasing him out of our lives.

We may begin at verse 1 by smiling at the fantasy of a talking snake, either pleasurably if like the Hebrews we can take that sort of thing or uncomfortably if with a modern supercilious taste we are not too sure that it ought to be in Scripture. But by the time we reach verse 6, if we have any sense and any sensibility, the horror of the human condition should be catching up with us. This scene is not about someone else, it is about ourselves. Far from having been banished from God's garden, we are not fit to be within a thousand miles of it.


## THAT ANCIENT PRINCE OF HELL

Genesis 3:1–7 (*cont'd*)

But there is more to the serpent than a mere personification of the process of temptation. It is not simply a fictional character like the fox and the crow in the Jewish fable.


(i)

The statement that it was one of the wild creatures that God had made is more than a device to tie it in loosely with what had gone before. In a real sense the serpent represents throughout this chapter the whole animal creation of the previous chapter, as the following table of correspondences shows:

| *Creation* (Chapter 2) | *Temptation* (Beginning of Chapter 3) | *Trial* (Middle of Chapter 3) | *Sentence* (End of Chapter 3) |
|---|---|---|---|
| man | serpent (= one of the animals) | man | serpent (= the animals) |
| animals | woman | woman | woman |
| woman | man | (serpent) | man |

For just now it is sufficient to point out that the story involves one of the animals in "man's" disobedience. As soon as the word "subtle" (it is actually very like the word "naked") is used of the serpent, we know something has gone badly wrong.

Not long since God himself had brought all the living creatures to the man to name them, and they had been pictured happy and content in the garden beside him. But his beneficent rule over them cannot have been so beneficent if one of them is now so keen to bring about his downfall. Even before the temptation scene begins it is clear that everything in the garden is not lovely, and that disharmony lurks just beneath the surface of its apparent harmony.

(ii)

We can probably go further still. By emphasizing that God had made this creature and that it was just one among the other animals in the garden, the author is implicitly denying that the serpent is a kind of Leviathan or Rahab, the "mythical" monster of chaos and evil whom his audience would know well (see the commentary on 1:1–2, *The dimension of evil*). He doesn't want a Satan or a Devil brought into the picture, in case that would be thought to detract from "man's" responsibility for his own sin. For that is above all the message he wants to get across, that Paradise is lost to humankind through its own fault and its own most grievous fault. No one else was to blame.

And yet—he calls the serpent *nachash,* which is not the only Hebrew word for snake, but is the very word that is frequently used of Leviathan and its fellows. See Job 26:13; Isa. 27:1;

Amos 9:3. Is he allowing in by the backdoor the very meaning his surface words deny is there? I have more than a sneaking suspicion that he is.

Having made his chief point that "man" must face up to his own guilt and not look for a scapegoat, he slips in a reminder that there is a larger force of evil abroad in the world as well, one that is independent of "man" and that has opposed God's will from the beginning of time. The battle which each man or woman must wage within himself or herself is but a small part of a much greater battle being waged between Heaven and Hell. That battle too must be won before Paradise can come on earth.

## THEY KNEW THAT THEY WERE NAKED

Genesis 3:1–7 (*cont'd*)

If we are to understand aright what verse 7 is saying, we must take it in conjunction not only with 2:25 but with 3:22.

(i)

If we compare it only with 2:25, we can easily go off at a wrong tangent. Nakedness suggests sex, and there is a long Christian tradition which sees sex as intimately involved with the Fall and at the root of what the theologians call "original sin". This tradition shows itself in numerous ways:

—in the idea of Adam's sin being transferred to all his descendants through inheritance, that is, through the act of procreation

—in the corollary arising from this that there can have been no sexual activity in Eden, and that this is what Gen. 2:25 is alluding to

—in the further corollary that the "knowledge of good and evil" must refer to knowledge of sexual matters

—in the readiness to accept that woman carried a greater blame for the Fall than man

—in the setting up of the monastic life of celibacy as a higher ideal than marriage (with some help here from St. Paul in 1

Cor. 7:9, "it is better to marry than to be aflame with passion", or with the AV, "to burn", but only just!)

—in the restriction of the priesthood to men

—in the anathematizing of birth-control, as if sex were not to be enjoyed unless children resulted

—in the sharply divergent standards of fidelity expected of the two sexes in marriage, as if women by their nature had to be kept on a tighter rein than men

and so on.

There is not the slightest shred of evidence for such prejudiced doctrines and ethical attitudes in this passage, or indeed anywhere else in the Old Testament. In Genesis Chapter 1 procreation lies at the very heart of the *blessing* pronounced on the animals and on "man" (verses 22 and 28), and the sex division is quite unambiguously included within the *imago dei* (verse 27). In this story it seems logical to assume that the animals and the man and the woman were meant to engage in intercourse if Paradise were to last any length of time, and that if the man and the woman had not been cast out of it, they would have had their children there. Above all, we have in the Song of Solomon an erotic and joyous celebration of sexual love, which in its explicitness and its essential cleanness is unsurpassed in the love poetry of any literature.

The Hebrews welcomed this world and its material and sensual life, and saw nothing wrong in a healthy enjoyment of all the "joys" of the flesh. It was only when sex was perverted to wrong ends, as in the rituals of their Canaanite neighbours, that they cried halt (see commentary on 1:26–31 (*cont'd*), *Male and Female*). If Christianity has been so frequently and so persistently obsessed with a flight from the material world and abstinence from the "sins" of the flesh, it is not due to the Old Testament but to an ascetic emphasis which only came into the faith in the New Testament period, and which has since been blown up out of all proportion, first by some of the things St. Paul said, later by St. Augustine and others of the Church Fathers.

It is high time that all this was brought out into the open and seen honestly for the aberration that it is. In particular it is high time that the doctrine of "original sin" in the sense of a sexually transmitted guilt going back to a primal guilty pair, was abandoned. Not only does it imply a belief in the historicity of this story, but it is not needed for us to be convinced of the universality of sin both in time and in place.

### (ii)

But to return to our passage. The equation between nakedness on the one hand and shame and guilt on the other has nothing to do with sex, but is to be explained in terms of the difference between a child and an adult. Even today in eastern lands little children run about naked, whereas adults clothe themselves. It is as simple as that.

There is a passage at the beginning of the book of Deuteronomy which beautifully illustrates this difference. It does not mention nakedness, but it does mention the "knowledge of good and evil". Moses is addressing Israel on the borders of the Promised Land, and says in God's name (1:35–40):

> Not one of these men of this evil generation shall see the good land which I swore to give to your fathers ... [but] your little ones, who you said would become a prey, and your children, who this day have no knowledge of good or evil, shall go in there, and to them I will give it, and they shall possess it. But as for you, turn, and journey into the wilderness . . . .

Little children are innocent, they run about naked, and they do not know "good and evil". The connections are so obvious that one can only conclude that they have not usually been noticed in the history of the interpretation of this passage in Genesis because the interpreters didn't want to notice them, having had other ideas of what it meant. We have seen what these other ideas were.

When therefore the eyes of the man and the woman were opened and they saw their nakedness, this simply means a quickly dawning realization that they were no longer innocent "children", but guilty and responsible "adults". They react with embarrassment and confusion, and immediately do what adults do, cover their nakedness. And it is not—repeat *not*—a single fig leaf that they use, something only to hide their sexual organs. The impressions of the great European artists painting this scene owe more to the teaching of the Church than to the text of Genesis. It is an "apron" made up of a number of fig leaves, in other words the normal clothing which one would expect early "man" in a hot region of the earth to wear.

(iii)

The knowledge which is "forbidden" human beings, that is, the knowledge which they in fact and in part possess, has then a double aspect. It is, as we have already seen, the knowledge of "everything", the kind of comprehensive knowledge which is in its fullest measure God's alone (see commentary on 2:8–15, *The trees of life and knowledge*). And it is, as we now see, the knowledge that distinguishes the grown adult from the child, the knowledge that comes with experience and education and responsibility and that inevitably involves selfishness and pride and compromise and cruelty and guilt.

At bottom the two kinds of knowledge are not that far apart, and this is the point of God's admission in 3:22 that "the man" had indeed become like "one of us". The innocent childhood of the human race has given way to the achievement but also to the sorrow and turmoil of the present day. Human beings have come of age, and to that extent they have truly joined the "immortals", weighed down with the governance of the world but, unlike them, quite lacking the angelic graces needed to cope. This is where "knowledge" has brought them.

It is not surprising that in the story God is pictured having tried his best to keep it from them. But in reality he has to live with the consequences as well as they. The predominant impression we are left with is of the heavenly Father looking on with infinite sadness and regret as his family grows up and seeing how, as in many a human family, this leads to the rebellion of the young and the splitting up of the parental home.

The successes his family have achieved with their "knowledge" are small consolation to him.

The lines have at last met. If when we try to restate the meaning of this story in modern terms, everything is not as neat and tidy as we would like, that is because of the story form. It is removing to the past and concentrating on an uncomplicated pastoral stage what is in fact the root cause of this whole complicated universe's present misery. That root cause is the strange mixture of ability and arrogance, of success and failure, of hope and remorse, of knowledge and guilt which is human sin. It has set an unbridgeable gulf between the human race and its Father in heaven—a gulf at any rate unbridgeable from its side.

## THE SIN DISCOVERED

Genesis 3:8–13

And they heard the sound of the Lord God walking in the garden in the cool of the day, and the man and his wife hid themselves from the presence of the Lord God among the trees of the garden. But the Lord God called to the man, and said to him, "Where are you?" And he said, "I heard the sound of thee in the garden, and I was afraid, because I was naked; and I hid myself." He said, "Who told you that you were naked? Have you eaten of the tree of which I commanded you not to eat?" The man said, "The woman whom thou gavest to be with me, she gave me fruit of the tree, and I ate." Then the Lord God said to the woman, "What is this that you have done?" The woman said, "The serpent beguiled me, and I ate."

In this scene God makes his first move to counter sin. He confronts the participants and demands an explanation. The order of trial is the opposite of the order of temptation. As the "manager", the man is properly arraigned first.

(i)

Nowhere is the naive language of "imagination" or ancient story more evident than here. God is the owner of the garden and goes out for a stroll in it in the evening breeze. He calls quite innocently for the gardener to ask how things are going. Only when he replies does he suspect that his instructions have not been carried out.

But for all the naivety of the scene, how very acute is the psychological insight! The man tries to be clever, suggesting a reason for not being at his post that would satisfy his employer. He didn't want to appear before him naked, since that would have been disrespectful for a grown man to do. But without realizing it he has given the show away. Then he blames his subordinate. It was the woman. And growing bolder, he even implicates his master ("whom thou gavest to be with me"). It is a perfect exposure of a guilty conscience at work. It should remove any doubt lingering from the previous scene that the man was not as guilty as the woman. She succumbed to temptation, but he grovels before God and dares to censure him at the same time. It's a despicable mixture.

The woman in her turn blames the serpent, but God does not question her further, nor does he ask the serpent to explain itself. At a symbolic level that would not have been appropriate. If it represents the animals, how could an animal be held responsible for what "man" had done? And if it is the embodiment of evil, a kind of Devil, might it not have encouraged the listeners to do what the author does not want done, remove the blame for human sin from "man" and put it on some extraneous force? The woman blamed the serpent in the story, but that is not to be "de-historicized" and used as an excuse for us to blame the Devil for our own mess.

(ii)

The replies of the man and the woman condemn them without any need for a jury to bring in a verdict of guilty. Just as unerringly as their statements and actions in the temptation scene they exemplify what the human condition now is. Fellow man and woman are mistrusted by each other, no longer in harmony. The animal kingdom represented by the serpent is also intimately involved. But chiefly God is feared, not loved, he is to be avoided or when he is approached, to be approached with excuses and pointing fingers and even a reprimand. The man and the woman are still in the garden, but Paradise has already vanished in a puff of smoke. The sentences to follow and the banishment after that are almost superfluous. Now begins the slow, sad exodus caught so finely in Milton's words:

> They hand in hand with wandering steps and slow
> Through Eden took their solitary way.

We might even with more fidelity to the Genesis story apply the magnificent but horrendous lines which Milton in *Paradise Lost* gives to the Satan cast down from heaven, to the man and the woman, that is, to ourselves:

> Farewell happy fields
> Where joy for ever dwells: Hail horrors, hail
> Infernal world, and thou profoundest Hell,
> Receive thy new possessor: one who brings
> A mind not to be changed by place or time.
> The mind is its own place, and in it self
> Can make a Heav'n of Hell, a Hell of Heav'n.

And that goes as well for the Arch-fiend's Promethean-like boast, spat forth from the infernal regions:

> Here at last
> We shall be free . . .
> Here we may reign secure, and in my choice
> To reign is worth ambition though in hell:
> Better to reign in hell, than serve in heaven.

## THE RECKONING—THE SERPENT

Genesis 3:14–15

> The Lord God said to the serpent,
> "Because you have done this,
>      cursed are you above all cattle,
>      and above all wild animals;
> upon your belly you shall go,

> and dust you shall eat
>   all the days of your life.
> I will put enmity between you and the woman,
>   and between your seed and her seed;
> he shall bruise your head,
>   and you shall bruise his heel."

After the trial come the sentences, pronounced on each of the guilty in turn. In the story, keeping up the fiction as it must, it is God who has to pronounce the sentences. But in reality what the scene does is to spell out the inevitable consequences of sin or rather, since the story cannot be too long, three appropriately representative consequences. It will be noticed that this part of the story is in poetry. Perhaps it survives in the "J" document more or less as it was in the original oral tradition, which if other cultures (e.g. Homeric Greece) are anything to go by would have been a poetic one.

The order of sentencing reverts to that of the temptation scene, the serpent coming first.

### (i)

In the allegory of the story it represents chiefly the animals of Chapter 2, of whom it is one, who are now portrayed as at loggerheads with "man". They with him are banished from Eden and with him have to live in the real world outside. Once "upright", they now "eat the dust" of the ground. This is nature "red in tooth and claw", hunted and dominated by "man" ("he shall bruise your head") and whenever possible, striking back to hurt and maim and kill ("and you shall bruise his heel").

It is the opposite of that vision of Paradise seen by Isaiah, to which we have referred a number of times, when "the wolf shall dwell with the lamb . . ." and if you like, the fox with the crow, but also when (and the prophet must have been thinking of this story)

> The sucking child shall play over the hole of the asp,
> and the weaned child shall put his hand on the adder's den.
>
> (Isa. 11:8)

The serpent, as one of the nastiest members of the animal kingdom, is in the fear and loathing it arouses in the breast of "man" a symbol of the continuous and unnecessarily bloody warfare that goes on between the two, and which cannot be God's will. Isaiah's language too is symbolic and should be read as an allegory, not an accurate description, of that ideal relationship between humankind and the animals of which we had a glimpse in this story in the heart-warming scene of 2:19–20, and which God wanted to develop when he created them both. It is as things should be, but are not. That they are not is presented as the serpent's punishment for its part in the Fall, but of course the major guilt attaches to the dominant partner, "man".

### (ii)

But there is probably another layer of symbolism still, or there would be in the audience's mind if they had allowed themselves to be "misled" by the term *nachash* used of the serpent in 3:1 — vague thoughts of the chaos monster and the chaos waters, of that greater power of evil at large in the world which the Old Testament personifies as Leviathan and the New as the Devil.

The story, as we saw, discourages this kind of speculation by reminding the audience that the serpent was God's creature, not his ancient foe of the primaeval conflict. But it is in the nature of such allegories to allow meanings to slip through even when they are directing the listener's attention elsewhere. The "prince of Hell" is not supposed to be here, but he cannot be kept out.

### (iii)

Remembering this, we should be wary about rejecting out of hand the traditional Christian application of this passage to the Messiah, the seed of a woman (Isa. 7:14; Matt. 1:23), who should in the end defeat the Devil and rescue "man" from his clutches.

Perhaps you have seen on television the "Service of Nine Lessons and Carols for Christmas-tide" from King's College Chapel, Cambridge. The sanctuary is dark as the choir enters carrying candles, a lone treble voice singing "Once in royal David's city". The Dean reads the preamble:

Beloved in Christ, at this Christmas-tide let it be our care and delight to hear again the message of the Angels, and in heart and mind to go even unto Bethlehem, and see this thing which is come to pass.

Therefore let us read and mark in Holy Scripture the tale of the loving purpose of God from the first days of our disobedience unto the glorious Redemption brought us by this Holy Child . . . .

The service is divided into nine readings with Christmas hymns or carols between. And the first lesson is Genesis 3:13–15, read by a choirboy and introduced with the rubric, "God declareth in the garden of Eden that the seed of woman shall bruise the serpent's head." It is plainly Christ and the Devil who are meant.

Just as plainly, this interpretation is illegitimate. The contest in these verses is equal and unresolved, and it is between the serpent and the "seed" of woman, which in Hebrew is nearly always a collective noun, referring to a man's descendants as a whole and not a single individual.

Paul's argument in Gal. 3:16 that "seed" (RSV "offspring") is singular is simply wrong. He is thinking of the promise to Abraham and his "seed" in Gen. 12:7 (RSV "descendants"), which he says is Christ. But his interpretation has been called upon to justify the application of the same word in this passage to Christ as well. This is not a wise thing to do. Both Paul and his converts in Galatia, or at any rate the Jews among them, must have been fully aware that his argument was wrong. However, they were both well used to this kind of Rabbinic manipulation of Scripture, and knew that it had to be taken with a pinch of salt. Paul is inviting his readers to say, "Your reasoning is false, but it's awfully clever, and we take your point." I wouldn't like to see such exegesis applied to Gen. 3:15, especially by literal-minded western Christians who have no experience of, or sympathy with, the techniques of a Jewish disputation.

There is then no prophecy of Christ's victory in this passage.

But there is a real sense in which it must, in addition to its more immediate meaning (where the serpent represents all the animals), be allowed to mirror both "man" and God's ongoing fight against the forces of evil in our and his world.

As Christians we know that the supreme battle in that war was fought and won by our Saviour at Golgotha, but this story of the Garden is not yet good news for humanity, and it should not be twisted to make it appear so. We will utterly ruin its force if as it sets before us the enormity of human sin, we read it with our finger tucked in at the Gospel's happy ending.

## THE RECKONING—THE WOMAN AND THE MAN

Genesis 3:16–19

To the woman he said,
"I will greatly multiply your pain in childbearing;
in pain you shall bring forth children,
yet your desire shall be for your husband,
and he shall rule over you."
And to Adam he said,
"Because you have listened to the voice of your wife,
and have eaten of the tree
of which I commanded you,
'You shall not eat of it',
cursed is the ground because of you;
in toil you shall eat of it all the days of your life;
thorns and thistles it shall bring forth to you;
and you shall eat the plants of the field.
In the sweat of your face
you shall eat bread
till you return to the ground,
for out of it you were taken;
you are dust,
and to dust you shall return."

The sentences pronounced in the story on (but in reality brought upon themselves by) the woman and the man are devastating. They home in with unwavering aim on the areas of life where each finds most joy and fulfilment—yet it is just there that the bitterest agony and misery await them.

(i)

When considering the woman's sentence we have to start with woman's actual situation in life. There never has been a time when her childbearing was painless, or when her status was not subordinate to that of man. In many societies indeed she has been little more than his chattel. Yet in spite of that her most ardent desire is for marriage and children. How simply the female dilemma in all ages is painted, and far more succinctly and far more honestly than in the more strident productions of "Women's Lib." propaganda. This little verse says it all.

What we must not do, however, is to take out of it any notion that woman's unhappy state is a particular cross she has to bear because she is particularly sinful. Our Victorian forefathers were fond of citing this verse as a reason for resisting the use of anaesthetic at childbirth and as a justification for not giving women the vote. We must reject out of hand such an obscene recourse to Scripture.

This is a story, not a treatise on morals. It is sketching lightly some and only some of the effects of human sin, and it is at this point concentrating on the female half of the fallen race. But it could easily have gone on to say that all disease and suffering, all slavery and exploitation, whether felt by or dealt out to male or female, have their origin in the same undivided guilt of humanity. This would have been just as true, but we would never have dreamt of concluding from it that hospitals or doctors or the overthrow of tyranny or the making of just laws were contrary to God's will. We must not give up trying as much as we can to alleviate human suffering simply because we know that it will never disappear until men and women both—and all of them—repent and are saved.

(ii)

In verses 17–19 it is the man's turn, and with the shrewdest insight the story selects its example from the realm of doing and achieving where the male ego is most vulnerable. Man had to work in the Hebrew Paradise. But here the picture is not of fulfilling labour, but of the unremitting toil of the Oriental peasant in the fields which was the lot of the bulk of humankind in Biblical times. It brought an aching that found no relief. It demanded a constant strife with soil and weeds and the elements. It ground his face in the dust and gave him neither dignity nor an adequate reward for his pains.

There are millions in our world today in the same boat, though we clever folk in the West have invented fertilisers and tractors (and, hypocrites that we are, we did not let Genesis stand in our way!). But are we really in any better case? Even as I write (in the summer of 1980), the unemployment figure in the Capitalist United Kingdom has climbed over the two million mark for the first time since the Thirties, a hungry and de-humanizing era we were sure could never return. Keynes and Galbraith had seen to that. And in Communist Poland the workers of Gdansk are on the streets protesting vigorously against conditions that their Marxist newspapers have been telling them for years only occurred in bourgeois, imperialist lands. Just who is kidding whom?

It is not God who has cursed the ground and made it yield only thorns and thistles (though that is the way it has to be put in the story). It is "men". Everything they touch turns to ashes, yet they still play God and delude themselves into promising everyone Paradise—tomorrow if not today. They can demand and they can promise, but they cannot deliver the goods.

### (iii)

And then comes death. Men and women both will return to the dust from which they emerged. It is a fitting end, for it is where they belong. Their ability, their achievements, their wisdom, their technology, above all their knowledge—none of these things entitles them to anything better. They cannot rise up from the dust by themselves. If they are ever to rise from it, it can only be by the grace of God. When they begin to acknow-ledge that, there may be some hope for the world.

## PARADISE LOST

Genesis 3:20–24

The man called his wife's name Eve, because she was the mother of all living. And the Lord God made for Adam and for his wife garments of skins, and clothed them.

Then the Lord God said, "Behold, the man has become like one of us, knowing good and evil; and now, lest he put forth his hand and take also of the tree of life, and eat, and live for ever"—therefore the Lord God sent him forth from the garden of Eden, to till the ground from which he was taken. He drove out the man; and at the east of the garden of Eden he placed the cherubim, and a flaming sword which turned every way, to guard the way to the tree of life.

The climax of the story is passed. "Man" is revealed for the rebellious and sinful creature that he is, and the disruption that has resulted has been luridly delineated. It remains only for him to be removed from the Paradise where he has never been except in a story, to the world outside where he has always been in fact.

(i)

There are subtleties in verses 20 and 21 which can easily be missed.

In verse 20 the man gives his wife a new name, Eve, which according to Hebrew tradition means "the mother of all living". But only a superficial assonance between the name and the Hebrew words for "life" or "living" (*chawwah* "Eve" and *chay* "living") supports this. The real thrust of the verse as we have it is negative. Life will go on and children will be born to them, but the relationship between the man and the woman has been permanently soured. He had in his joy in 2:23 named her "woman", but now a renaming is needed to reflect the nastier mastery which since the Fall he exercised over her ("and he shall rule over you," 3:16). Already, too, at the moment of his own sentencing (3:17), his own name had been changed from *ha-adam, "the* man", to *adam,* "a (mere) man".

Verse 21 is more positive. It indicates that God will provide for Adam and Eve in the outside world. It is, like the mark he puts on Cain in 4:15, an assertion that God's providence follows "men" into the darkness, protecting them and, more important, saving them from their own worst excesses against the time when he will act to reclaim them for his own. Here we do have the merest whisper of a Gospel to come, which mitigates the pain of humanity's exile. But it is no more than that, for the very provision God makes, animal hides instead of their own grass skirts, is an admission that the animals could now be killed by them for food and clothing. Again the sentence of 3:15 ("you shall bruise his heel") is being confirmed.

(ii)

The final three verses tie up the loose ends of the plot. Adam and Eve have not only to be banished from Eden to the cursed ground outside of it so that the sentences can operate, but so that their access to the tree of life, long in the background but now prominent again, may be cut off.

At this point God admits openly that by the knowledge they had gained by eating the fruit of the other tree they had achieved a par of sorts, not with himself, but with the angels or subordinate deities around him. He has to take steps to see to it that they cannot avail themselves of the fruit of immortality and "live for ever". They must die and so fulfil the threat he made in 2:17. So he not only "sent" them "forth" from the garden, but "drove" them "away" (this rather than "drove out" in verse 24) from its vicinity. They have still to "till" the ground, though it is an infinitely poorer soil. But their task of "guarding" (see 2:15) is taken from them and given to a phalanx of Cherubim who have a flashing and ever-twirling sword to repel them should they dare to return, from whatever direction they might come. Bereft of the fruit of life they can now only wither slowly and die like a plant deprived of water. The Cherubim are portrayed as the Hebrews knew them, as fiercesome warrior guards, half-human, half-bird, not the chubby "cherubs" which European artists in their ignorance thought they were.

(iii)

It is almost impossible to transmute all these details into a modern form of words, and perhaps we should not try too hard. But there are some things we can say.

"Man" is of the earth earthy, doomed to die like any other creature, but unlike them he has for good or ill—in the estimation of this story mainly for ill—caught the smell of heaven in his nostrils. With his ability and knowledge he is now intent on reaching there by his own efforts. He has in fact made himself into a god, and that is his undoing. There in his greatest ambition is his greatest sin, and how the world goes on suffering for it!

And what of God, who in the story tells a lie (or at least not the whole truth), who catches "man" out, puts him on trial, pronounces sentence upon him and now executes it? We are not meant to build up these features into a theology. The picture of God has to be de-historicized and brought into the present just as much as the picture of "man". When it is, we certainly see his anger at human sin. Even more we see his heart being broken by it. We also see him containing sin and holding it at bay. And there is just a glimpse of him preparing an answer for it.

But it is really "man" who holds the centre of this story's stage, for its chief theme, overriding all the rest, is of what might have been but for his sin and arrogance, the theme of Paradise Lost. Only we have to remember that it is a Hebrew story not a pagan story. This Paradise has not been filched from human beings by fate, but flung back by them in God's face as he offered it to them.

## CAIN AND ABEL

Genesis 4:1–2

Now Adam knew Eve his wife, and she conceived and bore Cain, saying, "I have gotten a man with the help of the Lord." And again, she bore his brother Abel. Now Abel was a keeper of sheep, and Cain a tiller of the ground.

The story of Cain and Abel, which takes up the first 16 verses of Chapter 4, may originally have been a separate story with its own self-contained lesson, but as we have it in Genesis it is an addendum to the story of the Garden of Eden, and composed undoubtedly by the same author. This is made clear by the repetition of much of the language of Chapters 2 and 3, notably "knew" in verse 1 and "know" in verse 9, "tiller" in verse 2 and "till" in verse 12, "keeper" in verse 9 ("keeper" in verse 2 is not the same Hebrew word as in 2:15 and 3:24), "driven away" and "be hidden" in verse 14, and above all "ground" in verses 2, 3, 10, 11, 12, and 14. There is also in verse 7 a whole phrase taken over bodily from 3:16.

The story gives us our first glimpse of "man" in his banished state. And what does he do? He murders his brother. Man and God, man and woman, man and the animals, man and the very ground he works—and now man and his brother. How much deeper can the rifts created by sin go?

(i)

As we have the story, it is not at all a full story like the story of Creation or that of the Garden or, still to come, the story of the Flood. It is the fullest of a number of small stories or, rather, bits of stories that we are given in the next couple of chapters— the episodes of Lamech in 4:19-24, of Seth in 4:25-26, of Enoch in 5:21-24, of Lamech the father of Noah in 5:28-29, and of the "Angel" marriages and the giants (Nephilim) in 6:1-4. But it is still no more than a torso. We would dearly like to know more about it, and indeed about all of these. But we have to make do with what we are given.

In the case of this story, what was it originally trying to say? Was it about the two kinds of life, pastoral and agricultural, represented by the two brothers? Was it about what constituted acceptable sacrifices, or about the institution of blood-revenge in tribal societies, or about a clan of travelling tinkers distinguished by a mark on their foreheads? Or was it about Israel's relations with the Kenites (Cainites), a tribal confederation that had been close to the Hebrews in the sojourn in the desert but had not entered Canaan with them (see Num. 24:21; 1 Sam. 15:6; 27:10)? All of these theories have been advanced by various scholars and argued for with more or less conviction. The plain fact is that we do not know.

Quite possibly the Hebrew audiences who heard the story were, at least in the beginning, conversant with the background and were able to fill in the gaps for themselves. But more important than that is the question why the author doesn't report the whole story for us. If, as I suspect, it is because not all of it was suitable for what he was wanting to say, then perhaps we ought not to do too much academic prying behind the scenes. It would be nice to know the background better, but it is not essential to know it. The author has given us what he wishes us to have, and we would be better advised to concentrate on that.

(ii)

The tone is set by the very first verse, where Eve's words should be translated "I have created a man *as well as* the Lord." There is a play on words between *qanithi* "I have gotten, obtained, created, made" and *qayin,* Hebrew for Cain. The word *qayin* apparently meant a kind of "spear" (2 Sam. 21:16), but that does not interest the author. He has something else in mind. The preposition which he attaches to "the Lord" is very odd. It is literally "with", which could at a stretch be rendered "with (the help of)", as in the RSV. But in my view he wants us to take exactly the opposite out of it.

Eve has just been thrown out of the garden, and her cry at her son's birth is intended to be exultant and arrogant rather than pious. She will show God! Not for her the thought of him alone giving life (2:7). She can do it too. She is in fact setting an example of defiance which Cain himself is later to follow, when he takes away life, something that was also the sole prerogative of God (Job 1:21).

The Hebrews didn't need to be told the meaning of Abel's name. It is one of the everyday Hebrew words for "breath" (*hebel*), though not so much the "breath" we breathe as a "puff" or "vapour". It is commonly used as a metaphor for something insubstantial, worthless, and quickly gone. Translated "vanity" it is Ecclesiastes' favourite word. We have it too in Job 7:16, "my days are a breath", and in Ps. 39:5, "Surely every man stands as a mere breath." There is no doubt that this name is in the story to underline the shortness and vanity of human life in general, and of Abel's own life in particular, cut off in its prime by his brother's hand.

### (iii)

Hardly is the story started, then, than the very names of the brothers offer their commentary on human nature. For the author that is much more significant than the other sparse details he gives us about them. Here is "man" but yesterday removed from Paradise, and he has learned nothing. Defiance in the midst of mortality! Could you get a succincter summary of his lost condition than that?

## I WILL BE GRACIOUS TO WHOM I WILL BE GRACIOUS

Genesis 4:3–7

> In the course of time Cain brought to the Lord an offering of the fruit of the ground, and Abel brought of the firstlings of his flock and of their fat portions. And the Lord had regard for Abel and his offering, but for Cain and his offering he had no regard. So Cain was very angry, and his countenance fell. The Lord said to Cain, "Why are you angry, and why has your countenance fallen? If you do well, will you not be accepted? And if you do not do well, sin is couching at the door; its desire is for you, but you must master it."

Abel was a shepherd and Cain a husbandman, and in due course each brought an offering appropriate to his vocation to set before the Lord, Abel some of the firstlings of his flock and Cain some of the cereals that he grew. The Lord "had regard" for Abel's offering but not for Cain's. Why was this?

### (i)

Most commentators assume that it must have had something to

do with the attitudes of the two men, and they find in the terse narrative just a suggestion that Cain may have been more perfunctory than his brother. It does not say that he brought the "first-fruits" of his crop, only the "fruit of the ground", whereas Abel did bring some first-born lambs. And there is a special mention of the "fat portions", that is, the choicest part of the animal, which in one type of sacrifice in the Temple (see Lev. 3:3ff.) was reserved for God and burnt on the altar. The Epistle to the Hebrews seems to agree with this interpretation, for it speaks of Abel offering to God "a more acceptable sacrifice" than Cain (11:4).

I am not convinced that this is being fair to Cain. We can presume that normal Hebrew sacrificial practice is being alluded to. In Leviticus Chapter 2, however, which gives the regulations for cereal offerings, it is not essential that these should be of first-fruits.

Moreover, Leviticus tells us that there was another and if anything more important type of animal sacrifice in which the whole beast and not just the best cut was consumed on the altar (see 1:12ff.). We should not get too clever in our search for symbolism in these stories. I don't think the author is at all meaning us to conclude that Cain was at this stage any less sincere than his brother in his desire to please God.

The chief emphasis of the passage is not on the offerings, which are quickly described and then forgotten about, but on God's response to them and thereafter on Cain's reaction to God's decision. As I see it, the whole point is that Abel's offering was accepted simply because God decided to accept it, and that Cain's was not accepted simply because God decided not to accept it. We are in the presence of that strange phenomenon which the Bible calls *grace,* the grace which "loved" Jacob and "hated" Esau (Mal. 1:2–3; Rom. 9:13), the grace which chose miserable little Israel rather than any other nation (Deut. 7:7–8), the grace indeed which found us and made us Christians and did not find our friends and relatives who are not Christians.

It is this free and unconditioned grace of God which Cain

cannot tolerate and which drives him first to resentment and jealousy and then to murder. Only such an interpretation seems to me to do justice to the context in which this passage is set.

(ii)

Cain in his refusal to accept God's decision therefore represents fallen human beings trying to do what it is not theirs to do: lay down the rules for their relationship with God. They want to know God's reasons for what he does, and to judge whether they think them satisfactory. And when he does not come up to scratch, they want to have the right to criticize and complain.

It is this resentment of men and women against the grace of God that God is intent on countering in the enigmatic words of verse 7 (which are in poetry; see the NEB). "If you do well" means not "if you behave yourself", but "if you accept my decision", however difficult it may be for you to understand. The next phrase, however, "will you not be accepted?" is, I think, a mistranslation. It gives the impression that if Cain accepts God's decision this time, then God will be bound next time round to accept Cain's offering. But there is no guarantee of this. That would be again to tie grace down to what "man" does.

The Hebrew is extremely cryptic, meaning literally "is there not a lifting?" It is clearly meant to balance the fact that Cain's face had just "fallen". But who is doing the lifting? If it is God lifting Cain's face—a common Hebrew idiom (see Num. 6:26 in the Aaronic benediction)—then the RSV has got it right. But it could be Cain lifting up his own face, also a Hebrew idiom, though not so common a one (but see Job 11:15). In that case the sense is "can you not hold your head high?" (so the NEB footnote). I much prefer this rendering. Cain is being counselled to take it on the chin like a man, and not to give way to pique and indignation.

For that way lies sin, crouching like a wild beast ready to spring. We are reminded of Peter's comparison of the Devil to a "roaring lion, walking about, seeking whom he may devour" (1 Pet. 5:8, AV). The third line of the poetic triplet is the same in

Hebrew as the third line of the sentence on the woman in 3:16. Just as in humanity's brave new world outside Eden a woman longs for a husband, though he may dominate her, so the demon sin has his eyes on the resentful man—or woman—but he—or she—has to dominate it!

(iii)

Perhaps the best commentary on this passage is Our Lord's parable of the labourers in the vineyard (Matt. 20:1–16). In a man's dealings with his fellow man justice is and must be the norm. Those who work through the "burden and heat of the day" ought to get a bigger wage than those who are taken on as evening approaches. But in God's dealings with "man" grace is the norm. Everyone who is given a job by him gets the same pay, however hard and long he labours or however easy and short his task. For where God's grace is concerned, no one deserves *any* pay, and comparisons are odious.

In the world of the marketplace men may justly complain if they do not receive the proper rate for the job. In the Kingdom of God no one has any rights, and complaining is sin. As the employer in the parable (and he is here representing God, not a model for a real employer) says, "Do you begrudge my generosity?", or in the more familiar words of the AV, "Is thine eye evil, because I am good?"

But the parable has a still crueller twist. It may be that some will be left standing idle even past the eleventh hour, because "no one has hired" them. For Jesus ends his parable not only with the words "So the last will be first, and the first last," but he adds (see the AV), "for many are called, but few chosen." Was the RSV right to omit this sentence because it does not occur in every manuscript?

This is one of the hardest lessons of all about God for us to swallow, that God chooses some and not others, that if you like, he has favourites. But accept it we must. "I will be gracious to whom I will be gracious, and will show mercy on whom I will show mercy" (Exod. 33:19). To do otherwise is sin, to take God's prerogative away from him and ourselves make the decisions. We see in the rest of the story of Cain what happens when a man does that.

## THE INEXORABLE MARCH OF SIN

Genesis 4:8–16

Cain said to Abel his brother, "Let us go out to the field". And when they were in the field, Cain rose up against his brother Abel, and killed him. Then the Lord said to Cain, "Where is Abel your brother?" He said, "I do not know; am I my brother's keeper?" And the Lord said, "What have you done? The voice of your brother's blood is crying to me from the ground. And now you are cursed from the ground, which has opened its mouth to receive your brother's blood from your hand. When you till the ground, it shall no longer yield to you its strength; you shall be a fugitive and a wanderer on the earth". Cain said to the Lord, "My punishment is greater than I can bear. Behold, thou hast driven me this day away from the ground; and from thy face I shall be hidden; and I shall be a fugitive and a wanderer on the earth, and whoever finds me will slay me". Then the Lord said to him, "Not so! If any one slays Cain, vengeance shall be taken on him sevenfold". And the Lord put a mark on Cain, lest any who came upon him should kill him. Then Cain went away from the presence of the Lord, and dwelt in the land of Nod, east of Eden.

Cain in a jealous rage inveigles Abel into a field and kills him. When questioned by God, he denies all knowledge of where he is, uttering the notorious words which could to the extremely sceptical author of this story well be the motto of humankind, "Am I my brother's keeper?" His mother Eve had glowed with pride in her ability to create new life. The new life thus created has grown up to disclaim any responsibility for his fellow man, and indeed to claim the right to do away with him should he stand in his way. For disobeying God Adam and Eve were driven from the garden to occupy a harsher "ground" outside of it, but for what he did Cain is driven accursed away even from this ground, and doomed to wander a fugitive in the land of Nod.

(i)

The language in verses 10 and 11 is both powerful and emotional. The verb "cry" or, better, "cry out" is often used of the appeal of the needy for help or of the oppressed for justice, either to a human judge (Gen. 41:55; 2 Kings 4:1) or to God (Exod. 22:23; Ps. 107:6). It is a cry and an appeal which will be increasingly heard in the new world. See also Luke 18:7; Rev. 6:9–10.

Here Abel's blood has a "voice" and does the crying for him. It cries from the ground which has "opened its mouth" to receive it. Behind this metaphor is the primitive idea of the god of death in other cultures devouring human beings with his fearsome jaws. In the Ras Shamra texts there is a picture of him crushing his victims in pieces and consuming "clay" (that is, human bodies) by the handful. Though there is of course no "god" of death in Israel's religion, the Old Testament often employs the idea figuratively, using the "earth" or Sheol as his counterpart. See Num. 16:32; Prov. 1:12; Isa. 5:14; Hab. 2:5. We even have in Isa. 25:8 the magnificently ironic picture of God at the last swallowing the swallower, a verse quoted by St. Paul in 1 Cor. 15:54, "Death is swallowed up in victory."

(ii)

But from this point on in the story the language is chiefly taken from a tribal background of blood-revenge (which is, of course, a different matter from supposing that the story had to do with the origin of that custom). According to this ancient code of the desert a wrong done to one member of a clan was a wrong done to it all. When it was a murder, the murderer had to pay with his life, and if his clan protected him, a blood-feud lasting many generations could ensue.

In this case, however, both slayer and slain belonged to the same clan. We have to imagine God as the chief of the clan banishing Cain as no longer fit to be a member of it, and we have to imagine Abel's other relatives (it does not seem to worry the author that in strict logic these shouldn't have been there!)

being dissatisfied with this verdict, and demanding full requital according to the code.

The symbolism is obvious. The killing and being killed of the Bedouin vendettas epitomise the murderous hatred of their brother man which fills the hearts of humanity parted from God. They are like the Bedouin Ishmael, Abraham's first son, "his hand against every man and every man's hand against him" (Gen. 16:12). And through this violent scene can be heard the plaintive and desperate cry of the innocent victims for protection and redress.

(iii)

The answer of Cain as sentence is pronounced on him is difficult (verse 13). The first word, in Hebrew ⁽awon, usually means "iniquity" or "guilt" rather than "punishment", as in the RSV's rendering, "My punishment is greater than I can bear." But it is the corollary of this translation that I really object to. It makes Cain whine and complain. One might think this suitably indicative of humanity's whining criticism of God. But I am not sure that it is right.

In Judges Chapter 8 it is related how the two chiefs of Midian, Zebah and Zalmunna, who had caused great havoc with their camel raids into Israel and had slain many Hebrews, including Gideon's own brothers, were at last captured and dragged before him. Gideon calls on his oldest son to execute them, but he was afraid, being just a boy. Verse 21 reads:

> Then Zebah and Zalmunna said, "Rise yourself, and fall upon us; for as the man is, so is his strength."

The two Bedouin acknowledge Gideon's right to slay them in accordance with the law of the desert, and expressing no regret and disdaining to plead for mercy, they tell him his duty to his face.

I prefer to think that Cain is being similarly defiant here. He has just been granted a reprieve from his just deserts. Not even he could believe he was being unfairly dealt with. But neither does he thank God for the reprieve. He accepts it arrogantly and stalks out holding his head high, showing now the stoicism he had been incapable of when his crime was first discovered. And he recognizes that the others in the clan will have to pursue him. The indignant whimperer has become Prometheus, disparaging the mercy he had received and quitting God's presence, brazenly prepared for his life of banishment.

The symbolism is not now of whining humanity but rather of human sin taking another giant step forward, as resentment gives way to insolence and effrontery.

I would translate verses 13 and 14 as follows (they are, I believe, also in poetry):

> My crime is too great to be forgiven (*literally* lifted)
> Yes, you have this day driven me away from the ground,
>     and away from you I must hide myself.
> I have to be a fugitive and a wanderer in the earth,
>     and all who catch up with me must slay me.

The sinner's hiding himself from God is just as relevant as in 3:10, but here there is the added fear that God may change his mind and exact the full vengeance of the tribal code. Cain is, it seems, ready even for that. It is the code by which he himself has now chosen to live, and if God can catch him, he may do his worst! It is not surprising that the next major story is the story of the Flood.

## THE MARK ON CAIN

Genesis 4:8–16 (*cont'd*)

Amazingly, however, God does not abandon Cain, but assures even this arrogant man, casting not a glance behind him, of his protection. This too is grace.

(i)

The background is still that of the blood-feud. But God is not now the chief of the clan mitigating the punishment which the murderer ought to have received. He is the "avenger of blood", the next-of-kin whose task it was to see that vengeance was exacted from the slayer of his relative. See Num. 35:19. That his threat was in this case directed against other relatives seeking Cain's life in accordance with the same savage code makes no difference. If they lay hands on Cain, they will have to reckon with him. And to make sure that they know this he puts a special mark on Cain's forehead, identifying him as still a member of his family, though he has lost all right to that status. We may compare the tattoo signs of primitive tribes and of the modern Gypsies. A similar mark of identification is mentioned in Ezek. 9:4–6 (on God's innocent ones) and in Rev. 13:16–17 (on the devotees of the Antichrist).

The "sevenfold" vengeance of verse 15 is to be taken figuratively, not literally. It is the typical exaggerated language of blood-revenge, used here to keep the motif going, not in the least to suggest that God ever takes more than his "pound of flesh" (or even that, if the truth were to be told).

(ii)

The lesson of this final part of the story is the same as that of Gen. 3:21 at the end of the Garden of Eden story, only this time it is more forcibly put.

Cain is condemned to wander a fugitive and an outlaw in the land of Nod. Our children know of this land as a land of dreams, the English meaning quite misleading them. But the Biblical Nod (the name means "wandering" in Hebrew) is not an innocent place. It is where, having scornfully rejected God's grace and mercy, "men" now live. This is what they have come to. It is a Hell of their own making, what Our Lord, in one of his most terrible metaphors, calls the "outer darkness", where there shall be "weeping and gnashing of teeth" (Matt. 8:12).

Yet even in this outer darkness, God's grace and mercy do not forsake his children. This is not the grace which chooses some and rejects others. It is the grace which sustains all his children even in their rebellion, and protects them even in their defiance, the grace that will not let sin and evil completely have their way. The day is coming—though it is not yet—when the two graces will be seen to be the same. For the few that are chosen are not chosen for their own sake, but for the sake of the many who are only temporarily set aside and only temporarily citizens of Nod.

(iii)

This is the fearful problem with which St. Paul wrestles in the letter to the Romans. He is thinking of the passing over of Israel, God's people of old, in favour of the Gentiles, God's new people. But in the larger context of Gen. 1–11 the problem is the same. In this context the whole of humankind, and not just Israel, has rejected its true calling. "Being ignorant of the righteousness that comes from God, and seeking to establish their own, they did not submit to God's righteousness"(Rom. 10:3). "But have they stumbled so as to fall? By no means!" (Rom. 11:11).

It is God's abiding purpose to save the whole world, but he has his own strange, even (to our little minds) offensive, ways of going about it. These are the ways of grace, and amid the lemming-like charge towards the precipice of perdition which sin in the person of Cain is now mounting, we are given our strongest yet intimation of them at work.

## THE GENEALOGIES OF CHAPTERS FOUR AND FIVE

Genesis 4:17–26; 5:1–32

> Cain knew his wife, and she conceived and bore Enoch; and he built a city, and called the name of the city after the name of his son, Enoch. To Enoch was born Irad; and Irad was the father of Mehuja-el, and Mehuja-el the father of Methusha-el, and Methusha-el the father of Lamech. And Lamech took two wives; the name of the one was Adah, and the name of the other Zillah. Adah bore Jabal; he was the father of those who dwell in tents and have cattle. His brother's name was Jubal; he was the father of all those who play the lyre and pipe. Zillah bore Tubal-cain; he was the forger of all instruments of bronze and iron. The sister of Tubal-cain was Naamah.

Lamech said to his wives:

> "Adah and Zillah, hear my voice;
>> you wives of Lamech, hearken to what I say:
> I have slain a man for wounding me,
>> a young man for striking me.
> If Cain is avenged sevenfold,
>> truly Lamech seventy-sevenfold."

And Adam knew his wife again, and she bore a son and called his name Seth, for she said, "God has appointed for me another child instead of Abel, for Cain slew him." To Seth also a son was born, and he called his name Enosh. At that time men began to call upon the name of the Lord.

This is the book of the generations of Adam. When God created man, he made him in the likeness of God. Male and female he created them, and he blessed them and named them Man when they were created. When Adam had lived a hundred and thirty years, he became the father of a son in his own likeness, after his image, and named him Seth. The days of Adam after he became the father of Seth were eight hundred years; and he had other sons and daughters. Thus all the days that Adam lived were nine hundred and thirty years; and he died.

When Seth had lived a hundred and five years, he became the father of Enosh. Seth lived after the birth of Enosh eight hundred and seven years, and had other sons and daughters. Thus all the days of Seth were nine hundred and twelve years; and he died.

When Enosh had lived ninety years, he became the father of Kenan. Enosh lived after the birth of Kenan eight hundred and fifteen years, and had other sons and daughters. Thus all the days of Enosh were nine hundred and five years; and he died.

When Kenan had lived seventy years, he became the father of Mahalalel. Kenan lived after the birth of Mahalalel eight hundred and forty years, and had other sons and daughters. Thus all the days of Kenan were nine hundred and ten years; and he died.

When Mahalalel had lived sixty-five years, he became the father of Jared. Mahalalel lived after the birth of Jared eight hundred and thirty years, and had other sons and daughters. Thus all the days of Mahalalel were eight hundred and ninety-five years; and he died.

When Jared had lived a hundred and sixty-two years he became the father of Enoch. Jared lived after the birth of Enoch eight hundred years, and had other sons and daughters. Thus all the days of Jared were nine hundred and sixty-two years; and he died.

When Enoch had lived sixty-five years, he became the father of Methuselah. Enoch walked with God after the birth of Methuselah three hundred years, and had other sons and daughters. Thus all the days of Enoch were three hundred and sixty-five years. Enoch walked with God; and he was not, for God took him.

When Methuselah had lived a hundred and eighty-seven years, he became the father of Lamech. Methuselah lived after the birth of Lamech seven hundred and eighty-two years, and had other sons and daughters. Thus all the days of Methuselah were nine hundred and sixty-nine years; and he died.

When Lamech had lived a hundred and eighty-two years, he became the father of a son, and called his name Noah, saying, "Out of the ground which the Lord has cursed this one shall bring us relief from our work and from the toil of our hands." Lamech lived after the birth of Noah five hundred and ninety-five years, and had other sons and daughters. Thus all the days of Lamech were seven hundred and seventy-seven years; and he died.

After Noah was five hundred years old, Noah became the father of Shem, Ham, and Japheth.

The Biblical genealogies are full of antiquarian information most of which is of interest now only to scholars. But if the ordinary reader understands broadly what they are about—and mostly they are not about real fathers and real sons—he can get quite a few insights into the Hebrew mind from them, and here and there a nugget of spiritual gold.

(i)

The second half of Chapter 4 is clearly part of an ancient Hebrew genealogy of sorts, though it lists more than relationships. The Italian-Jewish scholar Umberto Cassuto compares it with the opening lines of the Sumerian King List. The Sumerians were the non-Semitic people who preceded the Babylonians and Assyrians in Mesopotamia. The List enumerates all the known kings of their cities. There is no reason to doubt that the kings in the later part of the List are historical kings, but the nearer one gets to the top of it the less trustworthy it becomes.

Reigns are counted in thousands of years, and at least one of the names is that of a well-known semi-divine hero of Mesopotamian legend. The first eight kings are those who reigned—for a total of no less than 241,000 years!—before, as the List puts it, "the Flood streamed over the earth."

Cassuto draws attention to how the names of some of these antediluvian kings are accompanied by little explanatory glosses—"the shepherd", "the smith", "he who built such and such a city", etc. He thinks the source here was a Sumerian epic cycle of myths and legends, and that these glosses are a reminder to those who used the List of the fuller stories. The main purpose of this epic cycle was to relate the introduction in that primeval period of the civilized skills and trades—farming, shepherding, building, metal-working, music and the like—the features of "man's" life that marked him off from other living things.

(ii)

What we have in Gen. 4:17–26 and Gen. 5 are according to Cassuto Hebrew equivalents of the first portion of the Sumerian King List. The ancient heroes of Hebrew legend are brought together, presented as related to each other, and little notes are added to identify the fuller stories. The Hebrew lists probably served as an aid to the memory of Israel's story-tellers or "singers of tales". Behind them lies an old Hebrew epic cycle which reflected the views of the early Hebrews on the beginning of the world and the rise of civilization. In some cases the full story has been allowed into the Bible (the Creation story, the Garden of Eden story, the story of the Flood). In some cases it is only a bit of a story that survives (Cain and Abel). Elsewhere we merely have, as here, the list reproduced with its notes.

It was this popular Hebrew epic cycle that I had in mind when I said in the Introduction that the real "author" of Gen. 1–11 was the people of Israel itself. For it was this traditional lore that the Biblical writers used and adapted. The author of the "P" document, as we have seen, revised the stories rather more thoroughly than the author of the "J" document.

## LAMECH, SETH, ENOCH, AND ANOTHER LAMECH

Genesis 4:17–26; 5:1–32 (*cont'd*)

(iii)

The list in the second half of Chapter 4 is assigned to the "J" source. There may have been two stories about a patriarch called Cain in the older epic, or there may have been two separate patriarchs called Cain. Whatever the explanation, Cain is now no longer, as he was earlier in the chapter, a tiller of the soil who became a fugitive wanderer, but almost the opposite, the first man to build a city. From his descendants came Jabal, "the father of those who dwell in tents and have cattle", Jubal, the first musician, and Tubal-cain, the first metal-worker. Yet from the same family came also Lamech and Seth.

Lamech's story must have been a violent one, but all the writer preserves of it is a poem in which he exults triumphantly over the vengeance he was able to exact from his enemies, not for killing, but for merely wounding, and not just sevenfold (as in verse 15), but seventy-sevenfold. Did Jesus have this passage in mind when he said we should forgive our enemies to seventy times seven (Matt. 18:22)? See the RSV footnote.

Of Seth, apart from an explanation of his name, it is only recorded that in his day "men began to call upon the name of the Lord." This probably signifies the origin of organized religion. It is not saying that people in that distant time began to worship the one true God, but that they began to worship the host of gods whom they still worship today, but who we Hebrews know were in reality one God—the God of Israel.

There is very subtle preaching here. Bracketed together in one short list are three observations about "man":

(a) his great ability in the civilized arts
(b) his inordinate love of violence and conflict
(c) his recognition of a higher power.

"In the beginning" all three grew together, but the impression that is strongest on the reader is of Lamech's savage cry. He

rather than the farmers and engineers and musicians, rather
even than the priests and holy men, is the true representative
"man".

With a few swift strokes of his brush the author is setting the
scene for the catastrophe of the Flood, when, as it were in
exasperation, the Creator of the world asks "Was it all worth
it?", and is tempted to make an end of his Creation. We have to
listen very carefully to get his additional point that Seth does
not only stand for the origin of religion but, as his name
indicates, was a replacement for Abel who had been slain.
God's mercy is present too. Even in "man's" blackest hour there
is hope.

(iv)

Chapter 5, which is mainly from the "P" document, is a more
carefully composed variant and expansion of the list in Chapter
4. All the great men of the past were descended from Adam and
were in his likeness and image—this time literally. These first
men enjoyed huge life-spans, Methuselah's 969 years (verse 27)
being the longest, though none is anything like so long as the
reigns of the primaeval Sumerian kings. Compared to the puny
people of the author's day, the Hebrew heroes of old were men
indeed, but they were not kings, and they were not divine or
ever semi-divine. They all eventually died, as time and again the
genealogy litany-like dins it into our ears.

Or they all died but one. Enoch (verse 24) was mysteriously
translated. "He walked with God; and he was not, for God took
him." We have no knowledge of the story behind this strange
and enigmatic statement. Perhaps the Hebrews knew the story,
but even for them it is not allowed to become important. God
*may* in his grace have allowed a single man to escape the throes
of death, but all the rest died, and we belong to all the rest.

The genealogy ends with Noah. But who was Noah's father?
Not apparently Lamech the vengeful of 4:23, though he had the
same name, and probably ordinary Hebrews often confused the
two. This Lamech looked forward (verse 29) to his son Noah
"giving" him "relief" from his "toil" (there is a play on words

between the name Noah and the verb "give relief"). No doubt Noah did. But we are surely meant to take Lamech's words symbolically. There is a direct line linking the "toil" of the curse in 3:17 with the salvation wrought through Noah. All "men" are by nature like this Lamech, crying out for relief, and indeed like the other Lamech, crying out for revenge. But those who desire it and have faith enough can become like Noah.

The Biblical genealogies may be a bit of a bore, but if we know where to look, there are lessons to be learned from them.

## GIANTS IN THE EARTH

Genesis 6:1–4

> When men began to multiply on the face of the ground, and daughters were born to them, the sons of God saw that the daughters of men were fair; and they took to wife such of them as they chose. Then the Lord said, "My spirit shall not abide in man for ever, for he is flesh, but his days shall be a hundred and twenty years." The Nephilim were on the earth in those days, and also afterward, when the sons of God came in to the daughters of men, and they bore children to them. These were the mighty men that were of old, the men of renown.

These verses preserve a couple of scraps of ancient Hebrew tradition, possibly from the epic cycle we have just spoken about. They belong to the "J" document. They tell how some angels ("sons of God"—see the commentary on 1:26–31, *Let us make . . .*) married with human women and had children, and how at the same time there were on the earth a race of giants called the Nephilim. These giants were apparently still in Palestine when Caleb and the other spies reported back to Moses (see Num. 13:33, "we seemed to ourselves like grasshoppers, and so we seemed to them"), but they are not heard of again after that. The offspring of the Angel-marriages and their giant contemporaries together were the "mighty men that were of old, the men of renown."

(i)

There are many parallels to such stories in the "myths" of other nations. All ancient peoples believed in a Golden Age when men had walked and talked with the gods (compare Enoch in 5:24 and Noah in 6:9) and when the greatest men had a god as their father or a goddess as their mother. Achilles, the great Greek hero, was the son of a mortal king and the sea-nymph Thetis, the opposite of the children of the Hebrew story. But the point being made is not all that different. Men in these far-off days beyond recall were larger than life, what we weak mortals of the present time wished we were, but know we are not. And if they were not all half-divine, they were veritable giants compared with our little selves, like Hector, the great Trojan warrior, who was of human stock but was almost a match for Achilles.

The best commentary I can think of on all such stories is Prospero's lines from Shakespeare's *The Tempest:*

>           These our actors,
> As I foretold you, were all spirits and
> Are melted into air, into thin air:
> And, like the baseless fabric of this vision,
> The cloud-capp'd towers, the gorgeous palaces,
> The solemn temples, the great globe itself,
> Yea, all which it inherit, shall dissolve
> And, like this insubstantial pageant faded,
> Leave not a rack behind. We are such stuff
> As dreams are made on, and our little life
> Is rounded with a sleep.

All humanity's "myths" are like the "insubstantial pageant" of a play on stage, dreams to transport them out of themselves for a brief moment, but when the next morning comes and the play is ended, they have to awaken to reality's cold dawn. Even Achilles had to have his weak spot. He dies when the arrow of Paris, Hector's brother, strikes him in the heel, the only part of him that was vulnerable, since his mother had to hold him by it when she dipped him as an infant in the Styx, the river of Hades. The "divine" Achilles too was mortal. "If only" is the perennial message of the tales. They and their supermen are in reality no more permanent than ourselves.

But there is a lot more than wistfulness and pessimism to the Hebrew stories. The Angel-marriages survive in the Hebrew tradition not so much in order to give men and women something to dream about as to serve as a dreadful warning.

Though it is the "sons of God" who take the initiative, the end result is an intolerable admixture of the divine and the human. God has to take action. So he reduces the span of human life to a mere one hundred and twenty years. His spirit or breath would leave "men" then, and since apart from that they were but flesh they would die. No longer would they live the hundreds of years that the great patriarchs had lived. They were overreaching themselves and had to be cut down to size. We are still pre-Flood and not yet at the Psalmist's "three score years and ten" (Ps. 90:10). But as the garden with its tree of life recedes further and further into the background, we are almost there. It is as if God is admitting to a terrible mistake in having allowed the first man and woman access to that tree, and in having allowed their immediate descendants to have lived so long. It had left too many opportunities for things like these dangerous liaisons to take place.

This is a perturbing little episode that makes us feel uncomfortable for all sorts of reasons. But the real reason it ought to make us feel uncomfortable is the picture it gives us of humanity getting too near to divinity for their good. Other peoples' Golden Ages were vain illusions. The Hebrew "Golden Age" was a disastrous failure. Giant men meant giant sin.

It is possible to argue that since it was the "sons of God" who took the lead in the marriages, these were rebellious angels like Satan himself in the later Jewish and Christian stories, and that the author is hinting once again at the larger evil that plagues humankind in addition to its own sin and pride. If that is so, then like the association of the serpent with Leviathan, which he both discourages and encourages (see the commentary on 3:1–7, *That ancient prince of Hell*), it is no more than a hint. His attention at this moment, as all through these opening chapters of Genesis, is fixed unwaveringly upon "man" and his own responsibility for his fate. For almost without a break these remnants of ancient tales lead into the full and detailed story of the Flood, which comes on the earth because "the wickedness of man was great in the earth" (verse 5) and because it "was filled with violence" and "corrupt" (verses 11 and 12), not for any other reason.

## INTRODUCTORY TO THE STORY OF THE FLOOD

Genesis 6:5–9:19

(Readers are invited to read over these chapters before turning to the commentary.)

The story of the Flood is as we have it an effective enough but a very rambling story, now giving precise dates, now rather inconsistent in its details, now light and tripping in its style, now heavy and sombre. The main thrust of its meaning is not in doubt, but if we ask too many questions of it, its diffuseness begins to put us off. It comes as something of a relief to be told that it is in fact a combination of two stories, one originally belonging to the document "P", the other to the document "J", and that much of the evidence of the combining process is still visible, even in English translation, if we only look carefully for it.

It is well worth our while spending some time examining that evidence. Not only will we find it an engrossing exercise in literary detection, but having done it, we will be much better equipped to assess the spiritual meaning of these confusing chapters and their lesson for the believer today.

(i)

The key to uncovering the two separate stories is, as we might expect, the disposition of the divine names *Elohim* "God" and

*Yahweh* "The Lord", the first indicating the presence of the "P" source, the second that of the "J" source.

With the help of this key it is possible to distinguish a number of "doublets", that is, incidents that are told twice in slightly different language, e.g.

the divine decision to destroy "man" in 6:5–8 (with "The Lord") and again in 6:11–13 (with "God")

God's instructions to enter the Ark in 6:18–21 (with "God") and again in 7:1–4 (with "The Lord")

his promise never again to destroy every living creature in 8:21 (with "The Lord") and again in 9:15 (with "God").

(ii)

But more important than this we can now account for the many awkward discrepancies in the narrative. These gather round two main problems:

(a) *The number of animals entering the Ark.* In 6:19–20 in language that is reminiscent of Chapter 1 ("male and female", "according to their kinds", "creeping things") Noah is instructed (by "God") to take two of every sort in with him. Just after this, however, in 7:2–3, he is told (by "The Lord") to take with him seven pairs of clean animals, "the male and his mate", and one pair of animals that are not clean, along with seven pairs of every bird.

If we take these numbers in conjunction with 8:20, where Noah builds an altar (to "The Lord") and offers some of the clean animals and birds as a sacrifice, it is clear that the references to the seven pairs and the one pair and to a sacrifice both come from the "J" source, and that the references to two of every sort come from the "P" source. It did not have a sacrifice scene and therefore did not require extra animals beyond the breeding pair needed to preserve each species. (Neither source mentions fish, which could of course be left to fend for themselves!)

(b) *The duration of the Flood.* In 7:4 "The Lord" speaks of sending rain in seven days which will then fall on the earth for forty days. Thereafter in 8:6 we have a reference to the forty days ending, whereupon Noah despatches some birds from the Ark at seven day intervals to see if the waters had gone down. In 7:24, on the other hand, we are told that the waters prevailed upon the earth one hundred and fifty days and in 8:3ff. that at the end of these one hundred and fifty days they had hardly started to abate when the Ark grounded itself on a mountain. In both of these passages the divine name is "God". It is evident that the "J" version knew only the shorter periods of seven days and forty days, and that the larger number and the precise dates that accompany it (which agree if we count a month as thirty days; see 7:11 and 8:4) belong to the "P" version.

In "J", therefore, after an initial period of seven days' waiting, the Flood lasts forty days, and its recession takes the three periods of seven days implied in 8:10 ("another seven days") and 8:12. (Incidentally the raven, which was the first bird to be sent out, was an unclean bird (see Lev. 11:15), which is why there could not be only one pair of unclean birds as of the animals in 7:2–3.) In "P" the whole process takes much longer, lasting from the date 17.2.600 of Noah's life (7:11) to the date 27.2.601 (8:14), that is one year and ten days in all (the Septuagint by changing one figure makes this exactly a year). In the combined narrative the shorter periods of "J" have become simply imprecise intervals within "P"'s longer and more precise periods.

(iii)

There is a further problem with the Biblical Flood story which we did not have with the stories that precede it. There we adduced some external parallels, but they were generally indirect and remote. In the case of the Flood story, however, there exist direct and unmistakable parallels in the records of other ancient peoples. This raises the real and uncomfortable probability that the Hebrew story is a borrowed story. But before we look at that, I would like us to concentrate on the two Hebrew versions and see what we can make of them as stories on their own. We will begin with "P", which is the better preserved.

## THE "P" VERSION OF THE FLOOD

### Genesis 6:5–9:19 (*cont'd*)

(*Note:* In this and in the next section I make a few modifications to the RSV text to enable the narrative to flow more easily. None of these involves changing the original Hebrew.)

#### *Introductory notice* (6:9–10)

These are the generations of Noah. Noah was a righteous man, blameless in his generation; Noah walked with God. And Noah had three sons, Shem, Ham, and Japheth.

#### *The corruption of the earth* (6:11–12)

Now the earth was corrupt in God's sight, and the earth was filled with violence. And God saw the earth, and behold, it was corrupt; for all flesh had corrupted their way upon the earth.

#### *God tells Noah of his decision to destroy all flesh and instructs him to build an Ark* (6:13–22)

And God said to Noah, "I have determined to make an end of all flesh; for the earth is filled with violence through them; behold, I will destroy them with the earth. Make yourself an ark of gopher wood; make rooms in the ark, and cover it inside and out with pitch. This is how you are to make it; the length of the ark three hundred cubits, its breadth fifty cubits, and its height thirty cubits. Make a roof for the ark, and finish it to a cubit above; and set the door of the ark in its side; make it with lower, second, and third decks. For behold, I will bring a flood of waters upon the earth, to destroy all flesh in which is the breath of life from under heaven; everything that is on the earth shall die. But I will establish my covenant with you; and you shall come into the ark, you, your sons, your wife, and your sons' wives with you. And of every living thing of all flesh, you shall bring two of every sort into the ark, to keep them alive with you; they shall be male and female. Of the birds according to their kinds, and of the animals according to their kinds, of every creeping thing of the ground according to its kind, two of every sort shall come in to you, to keep them alive. Also take with you every sort of food that is eaten, and store it up; and it shall serve as food for you and for them."

Noah did this; he did all that God commanded him.

### *The Flood begins and Noah enters the Ark* (7:6, 11, 13–15, 16 (part))

Noah was six hundred years old when the flood of waters came upon the earth. In the six hundredth year of Noah's life, in the second month, on the seventeenth day of the month, on that day all the fountains of the great deep burst forth, and the windows of the heavens were opened. On the very same day Noah and his sons, Shem and Ham and Japheth, and Noah's wife and the three wives of his sons with them entered the ark, they and every beast according to its kind, and all the cattle according to their kinds, and every creeping thing that creeps on the earth according to its kind, and every bird according to its kind, every bird of every sort. They went into the ark with Noah, two and two of all flesh in which there was the breath of life. And they that entered, male and female of all flesh, went in as God had commanded him.

### *The rise of the Flood and the destruction of life* (7:17 (part), 18–21, 24)

The flood came upon the earth; and the waters prevailed and increased greatly upon the earth; and the ark floated on the face of the waters. And the waters prevailed so mightily upon the earth that all the high mountains under the whole heaven were covered; the waters prevailed above the mountains, covering them fifteen cubits deep. And all flesh died that moved upon the earth, birds, cattle, beasts, all swarming creatures that swarm upon the earth, and every man. And the waters prevailed upon the earth a hundred and fifty days.

(*Note:* The phrase "forty days" has been introduced into the first part of verse 17 from the "J" version. There is an indication of this in the awkward grammar of the Hebrew. The verb which I translate "came upon" does not mean "continued", as the RSV is forced to render it.)

### *"Hinge" verse* (8:1 (part))

But God had remembered Noah and all the beasts and all the cattle that were with him in the ark.

*The recession of the waters and the grounding of the Ark* (8:1 (part),
2 (part), 3 (part), 4–5, 13 (part), 14)

God had made a wind blow over the earth, and the waters began
to subside. The fountains of the deep and the windows of the
heavens were closed; and by the end of the one hundred and fifty
days the waters were abating. In the seventh month, on the seventeenth day of the month, the ark came to rest upon the mountains of
Ararat. And the waters continued to abate until the tenth month; in
the tenth month, on the first day of the month, the tops of the
mountains were seen. In the six hundred and first year, in the first
month, the first day of the month, the waters were dried from off the
earth. In the second month, on the twenty-seventh day of the month,
the earth was dry.

(*Note:* There may be some phrases missing at the beginning of
this paragraph. The point which the author wishes to emphasize is the grounding of the ark; the waters began to subside
before that, but not until then was it obvious that they had
ceased to "prevail".)

### *Noah leaves the Ark* (8:15–19)

Then God said to Noah, "Go forth from the ark, you and your
wife, and your sons and your sons' wives with you. Bring forth with
you every living thing that is with you of all flesh—birds and animals
and every creeping thing that creeps on the earth—that they may
breed abundantly on the earth, and be fruitful and multiply upon the
earth." So Noah went forth, and his sons and his wife and his sons'
wives with him. And every beast, every creeping thing, and every
bird, everything that moves upon the earth, went forth by families
out of the ark.

### *God blesses Noah* (9:1–7)

And God blessed Noah and his sons, and said to them, "Be fruitful
and multiply, and fill the earth. The fear of you and the dread of you
shall be upon every beast of the earth, and upon every bird of the air,
upon everything that creeps on the ground and all the fish of the sea;
into your hand they are delivered. Every moving thing that lives
shall be food for you; and as I gave you the green plants, I give you

everything. Only you shall not eat flesh with its life, that is, its blood.
For your life-blood I will surely require a reckoning; of every beast I
will require it and of man; of every man's brother I will require the
life of man. Whoever sheds the blood of man, by man shall his blood
be shed; for God made man in [*or* as] his own image. And you, be
fruitful and multiply, bring forth abundantly on the earth and
multiply in it."

### *God's covenant with all flesh* (9:8–17)

Then God said to Noah and to his sons with him, "Behold, I
establish my covenant with you and your descendants after you, and
with every living creature that is with you, the birds, the cattle, and
every beast of the earth with you, as many as came out of the ark. I
establish my covenant with you, that never again shall all flesh be cut
off by the waters of a flood, and never again shall there be a flood to
destroy the earth."

And God said, "This is the sign of the covenant which I make
between me and you and every living creature that is with you, for all
future generations: I set my bow in the cloud, and it shall be a sign of
the covenant between me and the earth. When I bring clouds over
the earth and the bow is seen in the clouds, I will remember my
covenant which is between me and you and every living creature of
all flesh; and the waters shall never again become a flood to destroy
all flesh. When the bow is in the clouds, I will look upon it and
remember the everlasting covenant between God and every living
creature of all flesh that is upon the earth." God said to Noah, "This
is the sign of the covenant which I have established between me and
all flesh that is upon the earth."

### *Final notice* (9:18–19)

The sons of Noah who went forth from the ark were Shem, Ham,
and Japheth. Ham was the father of Canaan. These three were the
sons of Noah; and from these the whole earth was peopled.

## STYLE AND STRUCTURE IN THE "P" VERSION

Genesis 6:5–9:19 (*cont'd*)

### (i)

The story written out above shows the same dignity of style and the same care in language as Chapter 1. Repetitions again abound. The pace is slow and measured like a minuet, being broken up at fairly regular intervals by an address of God or by the introduction of dates which specify not only the year but the month and day of Noah's life. As in Chapter 1 God often speaks directly, but in this narrative he is only once described as doing anything directly, in 8:1 (second half) where (reminding us of the moving of his Spirit in 1:2) he sends a wind to push back the waters. Otherwise things simply happen. The dates are obviously as fictional as the huge life-span of Noah (see commentary on the genealogy in Chapter 5). The purpose of the addresses and dates is probably to lend an impression of order amid chaos and of the stately progress of God's purpose as from a suitable distance he regulates events.

The Flood is made to last a whole year, which is clearly thought the ideal length for a cataclysm which is world-wide in its scope. It is as if the author is inviting us to witness the entire universe (as conceived by the Hebrews, of course—see Fig. 1), collapsing in upon itself and recovering again, and all the magnificent achievement of God in Creation being undone and redone. It is not therefore surprising that when God makes a covenant with Noah after it is all over and order is restored, it is in effect a covenant with the whole human race and with all living creatures, indeed with the earth itself, a point that is neatly underlined in the final notice that from the three sons of Noah "the whole earth was peopled".

Towards the end of the story there is quite a lot of theological strong meat as the author brings in some of his special priestly interests. But as in Chapter 1 he does not allow boredom to set in, but lightens things for his audience by a brilliant simplification. Just as in Chapter 1 the six days' toil and one day's rest of a normal peasant's week became a kind of parable of God's immense work in creating the world, so here the rainbow that shines through the clouds after rain becomes a reminder to a simple people of God's eternal goodness—or as it is more dramatically put for their benefit, a reminder to God himself of his promise never again to destroy the world he had made.

We can again only admire this old priest's mastery of his style, a style that allows him to entertain and to preach at one and the same time.

(ii)

Though the flow of the narrative is broken up from time to time and there are many repetitions of favourite words and phrases, the structure is not the regular panelled structure of Chapter 1 leading up by inexorable stages to a telling climax. The narrative in fact revolves around a "hinge". The hinge sentence is the first part of 8:1—"But God remembered [or better in the context, had remembered] Noah"—on each side of which there is arranged an equal number of paragraphs. There is even a rough equivalence of theme between opposite paragraphs, as the following summary table shows:

| | |
|---|---|
| Introductory notice | Final notice |
| All flesh corrupt | Covenant with all flesh |
| God's speech to Noah | God's blessing of Noah |
| Noah enters the Ark | Noah leaves the Ark |
| Rise of the Flood | Recession of the Flood |
| God remembers Noah | |

Step by step, as it were, the story pushes us down into chaos and bitter regret, and then step by step it raises us up to hope and assurance, making us pause on each step to make sure we take in what is being said to us.

In its structure as in its style "P"'s version of the Flood is, no less than the same document's story of Creation in Chapter 1, a composition of the highest artifice and imaginative skill. It may lack the "folksy" atmosphere of the "J" version with which in our Bibles it is now intertwined, and thus not have appealed so much to ordinary Hebrews, just as the story of Creation must have been less popular with them than the story of the Garden of Eden. But its original audience cannot but have been impressed by its marvellous fusion of simplicity with profundity. So ought we to be.

## THE "J" VERSION AND ITS STYLE AND STRUCTURE

### Genesis 6:5–9:19 (*cont'd*)

(*Note:* The "J" version survives in a much more partial state than the "P" version. It was also, it seems, affected when the versions were put together by a spill-over of some "P" language. Words and phrases introduced then are indicated by italics.)

#### *The Lord's decision to destroy mankind* (6:5–7)

The Lord saw that the wickedness of man was great in the earth, and that every imagination of the thoughts of his heart was only evil continually. And the Lord was sorry that he had made man on the earth, and it grieved him to his heart. So the Lord said, "I will blot out man whom I have *created* from the face of the ground, man and beast *and creeping things* and birds of the air, for I am sorry that I have made them."

#### *The Lord instructs Noah to build an Ark* (only 6:8 survives)

But Noah found favour in the eyes of the Lord . . . .

(*Note:* The missing portion would have contained a reference to the making of a window in the Ark, a feature not present in the "P" version. See 8:6.)

#### *The Lord instructs Noah to enter the Ark* (7:1–5)

Then the Lord said to Noah, "Go into the ark, you and all your household, *for I have seen that you are righteous before me in this generation.* Take with you seven pairs of all clean animals, the male and his mate; and a pair of the animals that are not clean, the male and his mate; and seven pairs of the birds of the air also, *male and female,* to keep seed alive upon the face of all the earth. For in seven days I will send rain upon the earth forty days and forty nights; and every living thing that I have made I will blot out from the face of the ground." And Noah did all that the Lord had commanded him.

*The Flood comes and Noah enters the Ark* (7:7–10, 16 (part))

And Noah and *his sons and his wife and his sons' wives* with him
went into the ark, to escape the waters of the flood. Of clean animals,
and of animals that are not clean, and of birds, *and of everything
that creeps on the ground, two and two, male and female,* went into
the ark with Noah, as *God* had commanded Noah. And after seven
days the waters of the flood came upon the earth; and the Lord shut
him in.

(*Note:* Verse 9 is the only place in the combined narrative where
a divine name is "wrongly" positioned.)

*The rise of the Flood and the destruction of life* (7:12, 17 (part),
22–23)

And rain fell upon the earth forty days and forty nights; and the
waters increased, and bore up the ark, and it rose high above the
earth. Everything on the dry land in whose nostrils was the breath of
life died. Every living thing that was upon the face of the ground was
blotted out, man and animals *and creeping things* and birds of the
air; they were blotted out from the earth. Only Noah was left, and
those that were with him in the ark.

*The recession of the waters* (only 8:6 (part), 2 (part), 3 (part) survive)

At the end of forty days the rain from the heavens was restrained,
and the waters began to recede from the earth . . . .

(*Note:* The phrase "at the end of forty days" was probably
originally in this position. In the missing portion the "J" version
would have had an account of the grounding of the Ark.)

*The sending out of the birds and the drying of the waters* (8:6 (part),
7–12, 13 (part))

And Noah opened the window which he had made in the ark, and
sent forth a raven; and it went to and fro until the waters were dried
up from the earth. [And Noah waited seven days], then he sent forth
a dove from him, to see if the waters had subsided from the face of
the ground; but the dove found no place to set her foot, and she

returned to him to the ark, for the waters were still on the face of the whole earth. So he put forth his hand and took her and brought her into the ark with him. He waited another seven days, and again he sent forth the dove out of the ark; and the dove came back to him in the evening, and lo, in her mouth a freshly plucked olive leaf; so Noah knew that the waters had subsided from the earth. Then he waited another seven days, and sent forth the dove; and she did not return to him any more. And Noah removed the covering of the ark, and looked, and behold, the face of the ground was dry.

(*Note:* The restoration "And Noah waited seven days" is required by the "another seven days" of verse 10.)

*Noah leaves the Ark* (nothing survives of this episode)

. . . . . .

*Noah's sacrifice and God's promise* (8:20–22)

Then Noah built an altar to the Lord, and took of every clean animal and of every clean bird, and offered burnt offerings on the altar. And when the Lord smelled the pleasing odour, the Lord said in his heart, "I will never again curse the ground because of man, though the imagination of man's heart is evil from his youth; neither will I ever again destroy every living creature as I have done. While the earth remains, seedtime and harvest, cold and heat, summer and winter, day and night, shall not cease."

Although not all of this story is recoverable from the combined narrative, enough is to reveal it as the same kind of deceptively simple folk tale as the Garden of Eden story in Chapters 2 and 3.

As there, the setting is localized and small-scale. The Flood, though obviously implicating the whole human race, seems in description to be not much more than a copious downpour of rain which lasts rather longer than usual. There are the same almost too human pictures of God—in Chapters 2 and 3 telling a "fib" and going for an evening walk, here being sorry that he had made "man", shutting Noah into the Ark, smelling the pleasing odour of Noah's sacrifice—and the same endearing and tender scenes, notably that where Noah sends out the birds, which the author lingers over so lovingly and uses so effectively to build up the tension of the plot.

We also have the same overlay of symbolism, though it is not so dense as in Chapters 2 and 3. The meaning is carried chiefly by the divine soliloquy at the beginning and the divine promise at the end, both of them only a few lines long, and not dispersed over nearly every paragraph.

The plot structure is a straightforward problem-solving one. The problem is God's, how to deal with the growing sin of "men". His solution—to destroy most of them, but to let a few escape. What this "historical" way of putting it means for a proper interpretation of the story we have still to consider. But meanwhile we can easily see how, though they may have admired the "P" story of the Flood, this one the Hebrews must have adored. It is to be hoped that we are not too sophisticated to share in their enjoyment.

## ARCHAEOLOGY AND THE FLOOD

### Genesis 6:5–9:19 (*cont'd*)

Following the excavations conducted by Sir Henry Layard on the sites of ancient Nineveh and Nimrud between 1845 and 1854 several large crates of cuneiform tablets were brought to the British Museum and deposited in its store-rooms. There they remained until a young English engraver called George Smith was taken on by the Museum in 1863 and given the task of arranging and piecing together the tablets. He equipped himself in the Babylonian language, which had just recently been deciphered, and set to work enthusiastically as both repairer and translator. It was some years before any beyond a few academics knew the importance of what he was doing. But when in 1872 he read a paper before the Society of Biblical Archaeology entitled "The Chaldaean account of the Deluge", the public at large learned that a Mesopotamian story of the Flood had been discovered.

The effect was nothing less than sensational. It was only a dozen years since Darwin's *On the Origin of Species* had appeared, and here was Genesis once more at the centre of controversy. The arguments raged. Did the new discovery prove the early chapters of the Bible true after all? Or did it merely show us the original "fairy tale" from which the Bible got its story? They are still raging today, though not so intensely and on the whole rather more sensibly—but alas! not so many people are interested.

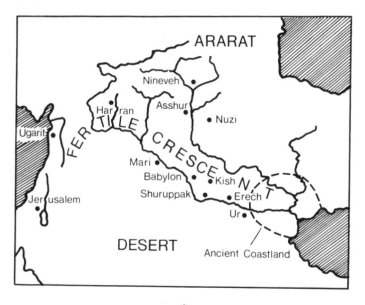

(i)

What is the archaeological evidence for the Flood?

In the course of his campaign at Ur in 1928–29, Sir Leonard Woolley reached a layer of clean clay and silt some three metres thick. Beyond this layer were purely Sumerian remains, while this side of it a more mixed culture was unearthed. He estimated that the layer had been formed about the middle of the fourth millennium B.C. (3,500 B.C.) by an inundation which he claimed was the Flood of Mesopotamian and Biblical story. Around the same time Stephen Langdon announced that he had discovered a similar alluvial stratum on the site of Kish further north near the city of Babylon, which he dated some centuries after Woolley's layer. And some time later another deposit was found at Fara, the site of the ancient Shuruppak, about halfway between Ur and Kish. It belongs to around 2,800 B.C. Each of the three marked a flood of some sort, and the archaeologists had a rare old time arguing which (if any) signified *the* Flood.

It is now agreed that the one with the best claim is that at Shuruppak, since in the Mesopotamian story the hero is explicitly connected with that city, being the son of its king. Moreover, such dates as the scholars are able to assign to the earliest known (real) Sumerian kings point us to the middle centuries of the third millennium B.C. rather than the fourth millennium where Woolley's and Langdon's deposits are to be placed.

This is as far as it goes a valuable finding, but only as far as it goes. The lower Tigris-Euphrates basin even today is notorious for violent inundations, and in fact takes in a huge area of land which in ancient times was still under the waters of the Persian Gulf (see the map on Fig. 2). The three of which the archaeologists have found evidence were, it seems, a bit special. Nevertheless, none can have been more than local in its after-effects. They would have caused immense destruction and loss of life and must have disrupted the economies of the areas for many years, but hardly more so than many other natural disasters in other parts of the world down the centuries. The one at Shuruppak seems to have fired people's imaginations more than the other two. But it looks as if it were these imaginations rather than what actually happened that were responsible for the great bulk of the popular story that was handed down.

It has also to be remembered that no Hebrews were involved in this "historical" Flood. They can only have heard of it through the spread of the Mesopotamian story. In that sense Noah has less claim than the son of the legendary king of

Shuruppak to historical existence. We would be well advised to treat him as, like Adam and Eve and Cain and Abel, a creation of Hebrew "imagination" and folklore.

(ii)

Archaeology has been even less helpful with the Ark than it has been with the Flood itself. Only representations and descriptions of small sailing craft have come down to us from ancient Mesopotamia. According to both the Mesopotamian and the Hebrew stories the Ark was a very large boat indeed. The Biblical boat was some one hundred and fifty yards long, about half the length of the great Queens of the Cunard Line. It is not possible to reconstruct it in detail from the information given, but it seems to have been little more than a huge floating house. The Mesopotamian boat was, as it is described, more like a colossal floating cube than a ship, and was considerably larger than the Biblical vessel.

When we take into account that the vessel had in each case to be built by the hero in a very short space of time and that it had to accommodate representatives of every living creature, it is not surprising that archaeology has come up with so little. It is patently quite impossible to take the Ark seriously as something that ever existed outside a story-teller's imagination.

This has not prevented foolish men from visiting eastern Turkey and having a go at climbing Mount Ararat (17,000 ft.) in the hope of coming across it. Every couple of decades or so we read in the papers that a piece of wood from it has been found or some debris from it sighted. None of these reports has survived serious investigation. As an article in *The Biblical Archaeologist* summed up one of them: "It may be regarded as a symptom of man's willingness to believe what he wishes to believe." In any case, it is only in the secondary Biblical story that the Ark is linked with Mount Ararat. In the primary Mesopotamian story the mountain where it grounded was called Mount Nitsir, thought to be much further to the south and east beyond the Tigris. Those with an ambition to discover the Ark should be looking there. But in fact, the story-tellers in each case probably simply chose a high mountainous region well known to their respective audiences.

(iii)

If in our short enquiry into the archaeological evidence of the Flood we have reached rather negative conclusions, that is because the facts of the case demand it. In other areas of Biblical life and custom archaeology has performed yeoman service—not least in illumining the background to the stories of Abraham and the other Patriarchs later in Genesis—and we owe it a great debt. But not here.

For in the end of the day we have to admit that neither the Mesopotamian nor the Biblical stories of the Flood are interested in history. They may go back ultimately to something that did take place. But in themselves they are both imaginative stories just like the other stories we have met in Gen. 1–11, and they ought not to have historical enquiries directed at them at all. It is a false trail. Only by examining them as stories shall we find out what they are about, and only by comparing them as stories shall we uncover what is unique about the Biblical one. We are back where we started—with George Smith's deciphering of the cuneiform tablet containing the Mesopotamian tale.


## THE MESOPOTAMIAN STORY OF THE FLOOD I

### Genesis 6:5–9:19 (*cont'd*)

The Mesopotamian story is now known in three versions, a Sumerian one in which the hero is called Ziusudra, a Babylonian one in which he is called Atrahasis (meaning "all-wise"), and an Assyrian one in which he is called Utnapishtim. There is evidence, however, from the text of these versions or from other sources that the same person is meant, and that he was the king, or the son of the king, of Shuruppak. I give some selections below from the Assyrian version, which is the one identified by George Smith and the best preserved of the three. The translation is my own.

This version makes up the eleventh tablet of the famous epic of the hero Gilgamesh. Gilgamesh is shattered by the death of his friend Enkidu and, brooding on the mortality of human life, he goes to seek advice and help from Utnapishtim in his home at the end of the world, knowing that he had survived the Flood and been granted immortality by the gods. His arrival gives the old man the chance to tell his story:

> Verily I shall open to thee, O Gilgamesh, a hidden matter,
> And the secret of the gods to thee I shall tell.
> The city Shuruppak, a city which thou knowest,
> On the bank of the river Euphrates situated—
> That city is ancient, and the gods dwelt in its midst.
> Their heart led the great gods to bring about the deluge.
> In its midst were their father Anu,
> Their counsellor the hero Enlil,
> Their throne-bearer Ninurta,
> Their inspector of canals Ennugi.

Anu was the god of heaven (the Mesopotamian Zeus), Enlil the god of wind, and Ninurta the god of earth (and of war). Ennugi was a minor deity, brought into this affair no doubt because of his office. Other deities mentioned in the story are Ea, the god of wisdom, Shamash the sun-god, Adad the god of thunder and his two attendants Shullat and Hanish, Eragal the god of the underworld, and Ishtar, the consort of Anu, a goddess both of love and of battle. Annunaki and Igigi are two general names for all the gods.

In this version no reason is given for the destruction of the world, but in the Atrahasis epic it is the clamour of human beings which the gods find insufferable, particularly Enlil, who as here takes the lead in bringing about the Flood, though as she herself later admits, it was the goddess Ishtar who first suggested the idea. In all three versions Ea appears as the hero's champion, and in all three he adopts the expedient of speaking to the wall of his hut in order to warn him rather than to him directly (it being forbidden to any god to let humans know the decisions of the gods).

Ninshiku Ea spoke [*or* sat] with them,
And their word he repeated to the reed-hut:
"O reed-hut, reed-hut, O wall, wall!
O reed-hut, listen, and O wall, understand.
O man of Shuruppak, son of Ubartutu,
Tear down the house, build a boat;
Abandon riches, seek to save lives;
Despise possessions, keep alive the soul;
Bring up the seed of all living things into the heart of the boat.
The boat which thou shalt build—
Let her size be measured,
Let her width and her length correspond;
Like the underworld ocean do thou roof her over."

Utnapishtim promises to obey, and asks what excuse he should
make to the people of Shuruppak. He is told to say that Enlil
has cast him off in his anger, and that he is condemned to go
down to the underworld ocean. He then sees to the construction
of the boat, which is a full acre in area, with six storeys, and is
covered over inside and out with pitch. Provisions are laid
aboard and a feast is held . . . .

Whatever I had I loaded upon her;
Whatever I had I loaded upon her of silver;
Whatever I had I loaded upon her of gold;
Whatever I had I loaded upon her of the seed of all living things.
I made go up into the heart of the boat all my family and kin;
The cattle of the field, the wild beasts of the field,
The artisans—all of them I made go up.
Shamash had set an appointed time, [saying]:
"He who sends 'destruction' at dusk shall rain down a shower of
  - 'hail';
Then do thou enter into the heart of the boat and close up thy door."
That appointed time had arrived.
He who sends "destruction" at dusk rained down a shower of "hail".
As to the day, I watched its appearance;
The day was terrible to be seen.
I entered into the heart of the boat and closed up the door.
When the boat was closed up, to Puzur-Amurri the boatman
I gave over the "great house" together with its equipment.

When the first rays of dawn shone forth,
There rose up from the foundation of the heavens a black cloud;
Adad thundered within it,
And Shullat and Hanish went in front,
They went throne-bearers over mountain and earth.
The posts [*sc.* of the world dam] Eragal tore away.
Ninurta came, causing the dam to follow.
The Annunaki lifted up the torches;
By their brightness they set ablaze the land.
The stillness caused by Adad reached to the heavens.
Whatever was bright they turned to blackness;
They shattered . . . . . . of the land like . . . . . .
For one day the south storm . . . . . . ;
Swiftly it blew and . . . . . . the mountains;
Like a battle it brought . . . . . . upon the people.
None could see his brother.
The people were not regarded in the heavens,
But the gods were affrighted at the deluge;
And they withdrew, they ascended to the heavens of Anu;
The gods crouched like a dog, laid down at the outer-wall.

Ishtar cried out like a woman in travail,
The pleasant-voiced mistress of the gods called out:
"The olden time verily has returned to clay,
Because I in the assembly of the gods commanded evil.
How could I command evil in the assembly of the gods,
Command battle for the destruction of my people,
When it was I myself who gave birth to my people?
They fill the deep like the spawn of fishes."
The Annunaki were weeping with her;
The gods were humbled, sat down with weeping;
Their lips were covered . . . . . .

At this point let us pause. The similarities with the Biblical story are obvious, but what of the differences? It is the din of "men" not their sin that brings destruction upon them. Like the Lord the Mesopotamian gods regret what they had done, but though it is in its own way touching, how revealing is the picture of them cowering like dogs, paralysed by their own power! When divinity itself was so hopelessly split, what hope could there be for humanity? We can feel the despair enveloping this story like a blanket.


## THE MESOPOTAMIAN STORY OF THE FLOOD II

Genesis 6:5–9:19 (*cont'd*)

The reader will have noticed that the Mesopotamian story is in poetry (and good poetry too). In this it is like most of the epics and legends of Israel's neighbours. We should probably conclude from this that the popular stories behind our present Genesis were also originally in poetry, and were chanted or sung to the people by their "singers of tales" rather than spoken. We think of Homer with his lyre or even of Chaucer's "Canterbury Tales", retailed among the pilgrims on their way to the cathedral to celebrate the Christian festivals. But to return to our story, Utnapishtim still speaking:

Six days and nights went on the wind;
The deluge-storm overwhelmed the land.
When the seventh day arrived, the storm-deluge subsided in the
    battle,
Which it had fought like a woman in labour.
The deep rested, the tempest was silent, the deluge ceased.
I looked out at the day; calm was established;
And all mankind was returning to clay;
The landscape had become flat like a roof.

I opened a hatch, and light fell upon my cheeks;
I bowed myself and sat and wept;
The tears ran down upon my cheeks.
I looked towards the world-regions at the edge of the deep;
In each of twelve places there rose up an island.
On Mount Nitsir the boat took stance;
Mount Nitsir held the boat fast, it did not allow her to move.
One day, a second day Mount Nitsir did thus;
A third day, a fourth day Mount Nitsir did thus;
A fifth day, a sixth day Mount Nitsir did thus.
When the seventh day arrived,
I caused to go forth and let go free a dove.

The dove went, she came back;
No resting-place appeared for her, and she turned round.
I caused to go forth and let go free a swallow.
The swallow went, she came back;
No resting-place appeared for her, and she turned round.
I caused to go forth and let go free a raven.
The raven went, and the drying up of the waters he saw;
He ate, he relieved himself, he croaked, he did not turn round.
I caused all to go forth to the four winds; I poured a libation;
I made an offering upon the temple tower of the mountain;
Seven and seven cult vessels I set up;
Into the bottom of them I poured cane, cedar, and myrtle.
The gods smelled the fragrance,
The gods smelled the sweet fragrance,
The gods gathered like flies above the maker of the libations.

Like the "J" version in the Bible the Mesopotamian story makes the most of the attractive incident of the sending out of the birds. The incident is not entirely invented, but is based on a custom of mariners in antiquity, who carried birds on board to use when they thought they were near land. The "J" version even has the naive picture of the Lord smelling the fragrance of the sacrifice, but its monotheism spared it the still cruder picture of the gods swarming like flies. The "P" version, rather more scrupulous in its language, misses out both the birds and the sacrifice scene, but there may be a connection between its use of the rainbow as a symbol of God's covenant and the "jewels" of Ishtar mentioned in the next few lines, though what these represent is uncertain.

As soon as the great goddess arrived,
She lifted up the great jewels which Anu had made to her liking, [saying]:
"Ye gods here, as surely as the lapis lazuli on my neck I shall not forget,
These days I shall consider and forever shall not forget.
Let the gods come to the offering,
But let not Enlil come to the offering,
Because he did not take counsel, but brought about the deluge,
And my people counted for destruction."

As soon as Enlil arrived,
He saw the boat, and Enlil was furious.
He was filled with rage against the Igigi, [saying]:
"Has some living soul come forth?
No man was to live in the destruction."
Ninurta opened his mouth and spoke,
Saying to the hero Enlil:
"Who if not Ea can make plans,
And who if not Ea can know every matter?"
Ea opened his mouth to speak,
Saying to the hero Enlil:
"Thou wisest of the gods, hero,
How without taking counsel couldst thou have brought about the
    deluge?
Upon the doer of sin lay his sin;
Upon the doer of crime lay his crime.
Yet be lenient, lest he be cut off;
Be patient, lest he . . . . . .
Instead of thy having brought about the deluge,
Would that a lion had risen up to diminish the people!
Instead of thy having brought about the deluge,
Would that a wolf had risen up to diminish the people!
Instead of thy having brought about the deluge,
Would that famine had been brought about to slay the land!
Instead of thy having brought about the deluge,
Would that pestilence had risen up to slay the land!
As for me, I did not open the secret of the great gods.
I (merely) caused the all-wise one (*Atrahasis!*) to see dreams,
And the secret of the gods he heard.
Now then do thou give him counsel."


Enlil went up into the heart of the boat;
He seized my hands and caused me to go up;
He caused my wife to go up and kneel at my side.
He touched our forehead, standing between us blessing us:
"Formerly Utnapishtim was a man,
But now let Utnapishtim and his wife be like unto us gods!
Let Utnapishtim dwell far away at the mouth of the rivers!"
They took me far away, they caused me to dwell at the mouth of the
    rivers.

This finishes the narrative of the Flood proper, but Utnapish-tim goes on to tell Gilgamesh about a magic plant which would restore his youth. Gilgamesh has to dive into the river to get it, and gives it the name "When he is an old man, a man is made young." But when he is carrying it off in his boat, he falls asleep, and a serpent (!) steals it, immediately sloughing its skin. The hero has to return to his own city, Uruk, without it.

## WHERE SIN ABOUNDED ...

Genesis 6:5–7, 11–13

> The Lord saw that the wickedness of man was great in the earth, and that every imagination of the thoughts of his heart was only evil continually. And the Lord was sorry that he had made man on the earth, and it grieved him to his heart. So the Lord said, "I will blot out man whom I have created from the face of the ground, man and beast and creeping things and birds of the air, for I am sorry that I have made them."

> Now the earth was corrupt in God's sight, and the earth was filled with violence. And God saw the earth, and behold, it was corrupt; for all flesh had corrupted their way upon the earth. And God said to Noah, "I have determined to make an end of all flesh; for the earth is filled with violence through them; behold I will destroy them with the earth."

The story of the Flood was clearly one of the best loved tales of eastern antiquity. It could be used by peoples of very diverse faiths to teach religious lessons, and it was elastic enough to accommodate them all. It is time for us to gather our thoughts on it together and see if we can isolate the lessons which the Hebrew story-tellers put into it. For these are the lessons that matter to us. They are not borrowed with the story, but derive from Israel's own unique apprehension of spiritual truth. The story was merely the vehicle for them, chosen by her story-tellers because it was so well known and had thus in a sense done the first part of their job for them, guaranteed them their audience's attention.

(i)

Fundamental, of course, to any attempt to restate these lessons in terms meaningful to our modern age is the realization that the story is *not* historical. As a story it had to speak about the past, but it was in reality speaking to the present. This was something the Hebrews sensed by intuition. Just as the Paradise of Eden was a place where everyone could live if they were not sinners, not where one man and one woman had once lived, so the Flood was not a catastrophe which an angry God had once actually brought upon the earth, but was a catastrophe facing the earth now as the story was being told to them. It ought to be the same for us. Our world is even as we read on the brink of tragedy, and for all his power God *may* choose not to prevent it unless "men" cease to arrogate his place and to practise the wanton "violence" endemic to their nature. So far his grace has held the cataclysm at bay, but it has cost him dear.

The first lesson of the Biblical story is then of the overweening pride of humanity drawing corruption and eventually destruction in its wake, and of the heart-rending problem which this daily presents to their Father in heaven.

(ii)

It is with that in mind that we should interpret the very human words used of God in 6:6. They are intended to highlight the poignancy of the divine predicament as he is confronted by human sin. God "was sorry" (*yinnachem*) that he had made "man", and "was grieved" (*yit'atseb*) to his heart. The first verb particularly is the kind that worries modern readers. We ask: Does this mean that God can change his mind, that he can one day appeal to "man" and the next decide to "blot" him "out"? Perhaps it does. But a Hebrew audience would not have reacted in that way.

They would be much more likely to think back to the etymology of Noah's name quoted in 5:29 (which they would know even if they were unfamiliar with all the genealogical details recorded in that chapter). Noah (in Hebrew *Noach*) was to "bring" his father Lamech "relief" (*yenachem,* but with only one *n*) from "toil" (*ʿitsabon*—it can also mean "grief", as the verb can also mean "toiled"). And the word "toil" would in its turn make them think of the "toil" (also *ʿitsabon*) of Adam's curse in 3:17, as indeed would the word "ground" (*adamah*) in the next verse of this passage. For all we know, the Hebrews may even have thought of the savage Lamech of 4:23–24. These rich overtones, linking Noah's very name with "man's first disobedience", if not with his insatiable lust for vengeance, are completely missed in English translation. In Hebrew they effectively balance God's human response with the human sin to which he is responding. The more the imagination of "man's" heart is invaded by evil, the more God's heart is broken. That, I am sure, is how the Hebrews would have understood this verse.

The Hebrews themselves were not unaware of the danger of using such a word as "was sorry" of God. Samuel could say to Saul in 1 Sam. 15:29, "The Glory of Israel will not lie or repent [*yinnachem* as here]; for he is not a man that he should repent" (the NEB in fact translates "that he should change his mind"). But in a story like this they preferred strong personal language to theological seemliness, just as in the story of the Garden of Eden (2:17) they were able to appreciate better than us why God is made to tell a "lie" (we might have quoted 1 Sam. 15:29 there too). For them only the most emotional of words could match the drama of these moments. By contrast, our intellectual quibbling only shows up our inability to see the wood for the trees.

There is an equally revealing play on words when some verses later (11–13) God intimates his decision to Noah. Three times we have the adjective "corrupt" or the verb "corrupted", and then God announces that he will "destroy" the earth. In Hebrew all four words share the same three consonants *sh, ch,* and *t*— *tishachet . . . nishchatah . . . hishchit . . . mashchit.* We question whether such language is appropriate for God. The first audience was helped by it to see that what God had determined to "destroy" was so "corrupt" that it was already all but self-"destroyed".

(iii)

This harping on human sin—and harping is not too strong a word—as the reason for the Flood stands in vivid contrast to the Mesopotamian story, where in one version no reason is given and in another it is the ridiculous and almost irrelevant one of the noise of humanity keeping the gods awake. That story reflects at bottom the unassuageable fear of ancient peoples faced with the violence of nature, which could at any moment sweep them and theirs away and leave no trace behind. No other reason was really needed. Human beings were the playthings of the gods, or of "fate", as we would be more inclined to say, victims rather than criminals.

The Hebrews too shared this ancient fear of the elements in a way that our modern scientific age can scarcely conceive. But they were not permitted to shelter behind it. They had been confronted by a God whose demands for justice and harmony and peace were all-consuming. If these things did not exist on his earth, it was not his fault, but the fault pre-eminently of "man", his highest creation. The conclusion was inescapable. "Men" were not as they were meant by him to be. They were sinners, now full-grown in sin, the innocence of Eden a fast-fading memory. If they did not repent and turn to him, they would ere long drag all Creation down with them to destruction and doom. God could not be blamed if he stood by and let them do their worst.

But, in the words of St. Paul, "where sin abounded, grace did much more abound" (Rom. 5:20, AV). The story of the Flood has only begun.

## ... GRACE DID MUCH MORE ABOUND

Genesis 6:8–9; 7:1

> But Noah found favour in the eyes of the Lord ... Noah was a righteous man, blameless in his generation; Noah walked with God.
>
> Then the Lord said to Noah, "Go into the ark, you and all your household, for I have seen that you are righteous before me in this generation."

Noah is the first clear example in Scripture of the man of faith, of an individual man who stands out against the crowd and goes God's way. Adam and Eve and Cain are representative figures, standing for all humanity in both its good side and its bad. We cannot identify with them as individuals, but only as typical human beings along with other human beings. But Noah, though a character of the Hebrew imagination, nevertheless emerges as an authentic person who by what he does differentiates himself from other people and leaves us an example to follow.

(i)

A cursory reading of what we are told about Noah might lead us to suppose that he was a bit of a plaster saint and that he was saved because he was good and his contemporaries bad. He was *blameless,* or as the AV has it "perfect". But the other words used of him carry in Hebrew the nuance of the proper attitude rather than of proper behaviour. Like the mysterious Enoch he *walked with God.* He chose God's side. And he was *righteous,* a favourite word of the Bible, denoting not the person who thinks himself or herself better than others (a debased meaning for which the conduct of too many so-called religious people must be held responsible), but the person who is in the right with God, who has the right attitude towards him.

But above all Noah had faith. He took God at his word and was not put off by what others said. He believed what God said about the coming Flood and he got down right away to building the Ark.

Genesis says nothing specifically about what the neighbours thought, but it will be remembered that in the Mesopotamian story Utnapishtim asks Ea what he should tell those who asked him what he was doing. Perhaps the "J" version, which is missing at this point, had a similar scene. But even in the story as Genesis gives us it we can infer the mockery of those around. The phrase "in his generations" (it is plural as in the AV) does not have the same word as "These are the generations of Noah" just before it. It could be better rendered "[the one blameless man] of his time" (NEB) or "[he alone was blameless] among his contemporaries" (Kidner). Compare 7:1. This gives us the necessary hint, and it is not difficult to picture Noah's neighbours saying, "Building a boat on dry land! How ridiculous can one get?"

In their utter simplicity these verses give us a perfect little cameo sketch of what real faith is about. It is about hearing God's voice through the din of unbelief and staking one's life on what one hears. It is about being ready when others are busy eating and drinking (see Matt. 24:36–39). It is about seeing danger (or hope) in the present scene where others can see only the same mixture as before. It is about that "assurance of things hoped for", that "conviction of things not seen", of which the Letter to the Hebrews speaks. Little wonder that Noah is assigned an honoured place in the great roll-call of faith in its eleventh chapter, where verse 7 reads:

> By faith Noah, being warned by God concerning events as yet unseen, took heed and constructed an ark for the saving of his household; by this he condemned the world and became an heir of the righteousness which comes by faith.

### (ii)

But even as we talk of Noah's faith, we have not yet penetrated to the deepest meaning of this passage. Before it is about the faith of "man", it is about the grace of God. The first thing we are told about Noah is that "he found favour in the eyes of the Lord." This is also to be included in God's response to the clamorous rebellion of human beings. As they went their way, mapping out their own destruction as they went, God chose one man with his family to go his way, to escape the cataclysm and make a new start. In this sense Noah is the first of that small band who down the ages are called out of the world so that eventually the world may be saved. He is the first with whom God makes a covenant (6:18), the harbinger of Israel, his covenanted people, and ultimately of the Christian Church, his people of the New Covenant.

It is not therefore surprising that the saving "through water"

of Noah and his family—"a few, that is, eight persons"—
becomes in Christian times a figure of the sacrament of baptism
(1 Pet. 3:20–21). Nor that in the writings of the Fathers and in
Christian art and hymnology the Ark becomes a favourite
symbol of the Church, holding out to her children the protection of the One who "remembered" Noah as all around them the
waters rage. As Pusey puts it in his hymn, "See round thine ark
the hungry billows curling . . .," but "Thou canst preserve us."

God's first act of grace in the story is the choosing or election
of Noah. But there is more to come, much more.


## EVEN THE RIGHTEOUS ARE SCARCELY SAVED

Genesis 8:21–22; 9:1–17

And when the Lord smelled the pleasing odour, the Lord said in his
heart, "I will never again curse the ground because of man, for the
imagination of man's heart is evil from his youth; neither will I ever
again destroy every living creature as I have done. While the earth
remains, seedtime and harvest, cold and heat, summer and winter,
day and night, shall not cease."

And God blessed Noah and his sons, and said to them, "Be fruitful
and multiply, and fill the earth. The fear of you and the dread of you
shall be upon every beast of the earth, and upon every bird of the air,
upon everything that creeps on the ground and all the fish of the sea;
into your hand they are delivered. Every moving thing that lives
shall be food for you; and as I gave you the green plants, I give you
everything. Only you shall not eat flesh with its life, that is, its blood.
For your lifeblood I will surely require a reckoning; of every beast I
will require it and of man; of every man's brother I will require the
life of man. Whoever sheds the blood of man, by man shall his blood
be shed; for God made man in his own image. And you, be fruitful
and multiply, bring forth abundantly on the earth and multiply in
it."

Then God said to Noah and to his sons with him, "Behold, I
establish my covenant with you and your descendants after you, and
with every living creature that is with you, the birds, the cattle, and
every beast of the earth with you, as many as came out of the ark. I

establish my covenant with you, that never again shall all flesh be cut off by the waters of a flood, and never again shall there be a flood to destroy the earth." And God said, "This is the sign of the covenant which I make between me and you and every living creature that is with you, for all future generations: I set my bow in the cloud, and it shall be a sign of the covenant between me and the earth. When I bring clouds over the earth and the bow is seen in the clouds, I will remember my covenant which is between me and you and every living creature of all flesh; and the waters shall never again become a flood to destroy all flesh. When the bow is in the clouds, I will look upon it and remember the everlasting covenant between God and every living creature of all flesh that is upon the earth." God said to Noah, "This is the sign of the covenant which I have established between me and all flesh that is upon the earth."

The crunch lines of the story are carried in the three final paragraphs, giving God's promise (8:21–22), his blessing (9:1–7), and his covenant (9:8–17). God would be no less than just if he here and now made an end of this corrupt earth and its corrupt inhabitants. But in his grace he does not.

(i)

At this level Noah *is* like Adam and Cain. He is "Everyman", standing for the whole human race who do not realize how near they have come to turning God's love into bitter and final judgment, yet who through his grace are not consumed. For the promise is not simply to those who escaped from the Flood, though it has to be put that way in the story. It is to all human beings, evil though the imagination of their hearts may be. By saying that God will not again destroy every living creature, the promise says in reality that he never intended to. As long as the earth remains the seasons will return in their time and the miracle of a new dawn will happen every day. He is in control of nature's fierce floods, and will not allow them to overstep the bounds he has set for them.

The covenant too is with all flesh, corrupt as it is, indeed with all Creation, not like the covenant of Sinai only with God's chosen people. It is not an agreement which he did not make with them at the very beginning, but is on the contrary one that is written into the very constitution of things. His grace and providence will overshadow sinful humanity as surely as the rainbow follows the storm. It is only in the story that the rainbow is created now. The Hebrews knew and we know that it has always been there.

Divested of its historical trappings, the deepest lesson of the Flood story is not that the wicked are going to be destroyed and that only the righteous will be saved. It is, in the words of the apostle (1 Pet. 4:18)—quoting a verse from Proverbs, but in the Septuagint version—that *even the righteous are scarcely saved* (AV). But in fact not only they but all "men" are, and one day this will be seen to be so, and the world of "men" will become as it ought to be. In the meanwhile God will not suffer their pride and sin to thwart his purpose.

Say this as I have said it and it smacks of a truism, utterly without bite. God is good and God is sovereign, therefore he will not let sin stand in his way. But put it, as the authors of Genesis did, in a picturesque and compelling story, and we see that it is anything but. The abounding grace of God gets the adoration it deserves. In their skilful hands this apparently naive story, not even original to the Hebrews, sets forth the very salutary theological lesson that only a hair's breadth separates God's justice and his mercy. By relating how in an imaginary past his wrath very nearly triumphed over his love, it forcibly reminds us that this is still the case.

(ii)

There is nothing like this in the Mesopotamian story. It began with despair and it ends with despair. Nature still menaces humanity and divinity is still divided. Pathetically the gods gather like flies around Utnapishtim's sacrifice as though relieved that their own savagery had been for the moment tamed.

The scene that ensues between Ishtar and Enlil and Ea is a moving one in its own way. The goddess had been earlier stricken with remorse that she had commanded the destruction of her people, and now she undertakes never to forget what had happened, but it is beyond her power to guarantee that it would not happen again. She is in fact afraid of Enlil, and tries to keep the knowledge of Utnapishtim's escape from him. And with good cause—for when Enlil arrives he is livid with rage to discover that someone had survived. "No man was to live in the destruction." Ninurta points the finger at Ea, the gentle god who had warned Utnapishtim, and he is forced to speak. He takes Enlil to task—but respectfully—for his cruelty. He should have punished only the guilty, not the whole of humankind, and was it not in any case a god's duty to be lenient and patient? But he too is afraid of Enlil, as his words excusing his own part in the affair show. In the end all he can suggest is that Enlil visit Utnapishtim and discuss with him what should be done. A dramatic scene, beautifully portrayed, but what discord there is in that heaven!

Enlil agrees to visit Utnapishtim. But what is his solution? He confers immortality on him and then removes him as far away from the rest of humankind as possible (in this story too they are still there, though they are supposed to have been destroyed!). There is not a particle of hope for the audience beyond perhaps the chance that they will find a good god like Ea to look after them. The granting of immortality to one person in the past, and to one person only, serves if anything to underline the mortality of all the rest of them—and Gilgamesh's failure to cash in on Utnapishtim's good fortune merely rubs in the message further.

Nor, as we have seen, is anything said throughout the story about "man's" sin and pride, and therefore about the possibility of change should he repent. An almost unrelieved pessimism pervades it to its bitter ending. "Man" is the toy of the fates, the fates themselves are constantly bickering, and the kindly fates have an almost impossible task keeping their more vicious colleagues in check. It has a whiff of Prometheus about it, as human beings are left to rail helplessly against heaven. But where is the Gospel that they so desperately need?

## OUR GOD IS A CONSUMING FIRE

Genesis 8:21–22; 9:1–17 (*cont'd*)

(iii)

In sharpest contradistinction the Hebrew story issues in hope. It does contain a Gospel. But let us beware lest we take it too lightly! The hope which this story holds out is a frighteningly realistic hope, the Gospel it preaches indeed a straw for a drowning man to clutch.

In between the promise and the covenant comes the blessing (9:1–7). But can we honestly call it a blessing?

We would be very foolish to regard this perturbing passage as in any way describing a state of affairs with which either God or ourselves can remain content. The animal creation, once "man's" companions, now go in fear and dread of him. They are delivered into his hand to be killed for his food (with the added Hebrew touch that the blood must not be eaten along with the flesh). This is the reality which Chapter 1 could not bring itself to put into its account of Creation, and which it could only allude to obliquely (see the commentary on 1:26–31, *I have given every green plant*). It is the reality of "man's" rule over Creation gone sour. "I give you everything" in verse 3 must be shatteringly ironic.

The same goes for "man's" relations with his fellows. That "man" now kills his brother as well as the animals is recognized in the statement that "whoever sheds the blood of man, by man shall his blood be shed" (verse 6). This is not to my mind meant to be a legal sanction against murder or a justification for capital punishment—there is no mention of other human beings requiring a reckoning, but only of God requiring it. In this context it is more of a sad admission on God's part that his creatures regard human life as infinitely less precious than he does. "Man" had been created to be his viceroy, his ambassador, and his person ought to be inviolable (see further *A note on the "image" in the New Testament* in the commentary on 1:26–31). But alas! it is not. It is as if the Flood had never happened.

And that is just the point. The Flood did not happen. All through this so-called blessing, God is not addressing a righteous remnant but all of us as we are. The blessing in it does not consist in allowing us (with one exception) to do what in fact we do every day anyway, but in its hidden hint that while we continue doing these things God is nevertheless in charge. It is against this awful background of an arrogant and unredeemed humanity and a violent, feuding universe that life goes on until in his own good time (or is it when he can?) an angry and a grieving but a still gracious God works out his great salvation.

(iv)

We perhaps see now how preposterous a thing is a faith like Noah's. The cloying and sentimental piety we call faith would not save a titmouse. There is just a chance that a faith like Noah's may yet tip the scales on the side of God's grace and save a world.

I leave the last word on the story of the Flood to two passages of Scripture which taken together seem to me to sum up succinctly but potently its abiding but double-edged message.

First from the Psalms:

> It is he who remembered us in our low estate,
>   for his steadfast love endures for ever;
> and rescued us from our foes,
>   for his steadfast love endures for ever;
> he who gives food to all flesh,
>   for his steadfast love endures for ever.

(Ps. 136:23–25)

And second from the writer of the Epistle to the Hebrews, who of all the New Testament writers has perhaps most sensitively entered into the spirit of this part of the Old Testament:

See that you do not refuse him who is speaking. For if they did not escape when they refused him who warned them on earth, much less shall we escape if we reject him who warns from heaven. His voice then shook the earth; but now he has promised, "Yet once more I will shake not only the earth but also the heaven." This phrase, "Yet once more", indicates the removal of what is shaken, as of what has been made, in order that what cannot be shaken may remain. Therefore let us be grateful for receiving a kingdom that cannot be shaken, and thus let us offer to God acceptable worship, with reverence and awe; for our God is a consuming fire.

(Heb. 12:25–29)

## THOUGHTS ON THE HEBREW TABLE OF THE NATIONS I

### Genesis 9:20–29; 10:1–32

Noah was the first tiller of the soil. He planted a vineyard; and he drank of the wine, and became drunk, and lay uncovered in his tent. And Ham, the father of Canaan, saw the nakedness of his father, and told his two brothers outside. Then Shem and Japheth took a garment, laid it upon both their shoulders, and walked backward and covered the nakedness of their father; their faces were turned away, and they did not see their father's nakedness. When Noah awoke from his wine and knew what his youngest son had done to him, he said,

"Cursed be Canaan;
a slave of slaves shall he be to his brothers."

He also said,

"Blessed by the Lord my God be Shem;
and let Canaan be his slave.
God enlarge Japheth,
and let him dwell in the tents of Shem;
and let Canaan be his slave."

After the flood Noah lived three hundred and fifty years. All the days of Noah were nine hundred and fifty years; and he died.

These are the generations of the sons of Noah, Shem, Ham, and Japheth; sons were born to them after the flood.

The sons of Japheth: Gomer, Magog, Madai, Javan, Tubal, Meshech, and Tiras. The sons of Gomer: Ashkenaz, Riphath, and Togarmah. The sons of Javan: Elishah, Tarshish, Kittim, and Dodanim. From these the coastland peoples spread. These are the sons of Japheth in their lands, each with his own language, by their families, in their nations.

The sons of Ham: Cush, Egypt, Put, and Canaan. The sons of Cush: Seba, Havilah, Sabtah, Raamah, and Sabteca. The sons of Raamah: Sheba and Dedan. Cush became the father of Nimrod; he was the first on earth to be a mighty man. He was a mighty hunter before the Lord; therefore it is said, "Like Nimrod a mighty hunter before the Lord." The beginning of his kingdom was Babel, Erech, and Accad, all of them in the land of Shinar. From that land he went to Assyria, and built Nineveh, Rehoboth-Ir, Calah, and Resen between Nineveh and Calah; that is the great city. Egypt became the father of Ludim, Anamim, Lehabim, Naph-tuhim, Pathrusim, Casluhim (whence came the Philistines), and Caphtorim.

Canaan became the father of Sidon his first-born, and Heth, and the Jebusites, the Amorites, the Girgashites, the Hivites, the Arkites, the Sinites, the Arvadites, the Zemarites, and the Hamathites. Afterward the families of the Canaanites spread abroad. And the territory of the Canaanites extended from Sidon, in the direction of Gerar, as far as Gaza, and in the direction of Sodom, Gomorrah, Admah, and Zeboi-im, as far as Lasha. These are the sons of Ham, by their families, their languages, their lands, and their nations.

To Shem also, the father of all the children of Eber, the elder brother of Japheth, children were born. The sons of Shem: Elam, Asshur, Arpachshad, Lud, and Aram. The sons of Aram: Uz, Hul, Gether, and Mash. Arpachshad became the father of Shelah; and Shelah became the father of Eber. To Eber were born two sons: the name of the one was Peleg, for in his days the earth was divided, and his brother's name was Joktan. Joktan became the father of Almodad, Sheleph, Hazarmaveth, Jerah, Hadoram, Uzal, Diklah, Obal, Abima-el, Sheba, Ophir, Havilah, and Jobab; all these were the sons of Joktan. The territory in which they lived extended from Mesha in the direction of Sephar to the hill country of the east. These are the sons of Shem, by their families, their languages, their lands, and their nations.

These are the families of the sons of Noah, according to their genealogies, in their nations; and from these the nations spread abroad on the earth after the flood.

The nasty little story at the end of Chapter 9 belongs (as a kind of expanded gloss) with the genealogy in Chapter 10 rather than with the Flood story. The material in these one and a half chapters is taken from both the documents "J" and "P", but it is of the same kind. It divides up the world of the Hebrews among the descendants of Noah in the form of a family tree. In other words, the great majority of the names are not individual names but stand for ethnic groups or geographical areas.

It is as if, in Bruce Vawter's neat analogy, we were to record our history in the following fashion: "The descendants of Europe: Britain, France, Spain . . . Britain became the father of America, Canada . . . To Spain also children were born: California, Mexico . . . The descendants of America: Virginia, Georgia, Carolina . . . Georgia became the father of Atlanta, Augusta, Savannah . . . ," and so forth. And, it could be added, as if at the same time we were to compose little stories to sum up important events and record our opinion of the participants.

(i)

We have the same problem with Noah here as we had with Cain in Chapter 4, who after he had become a nomadic fugitive is supposed to have founded a city. In the story in 9:20ff. the hero of the Flood, the shining example of faith to succeeding generations, becomes overnight the discoverer of wine, the first to plant a vineyard, and the first to get himself outrageously drunk. How could these descriptions be of the same person? To us the ironical message is obvious. Even after the Flood humanity is much the same. And there may be more irony still. Is it being suggested that the wine which makes them forget their sorrows is the relief from toil which in 5:29 old Lamech had longed for his son to bring him? Or is wine being set forth as an allegory or parable of human civilization as a whole, now beneficial, now disastrous in its effects?

(ii)

Chiefly, however, this story is saying something important to the Hebrews about the peoples whom the three brothers represent. As Noah is sprawling naked his son Ham sees him and tells his two brothers, who—but without looking—cover

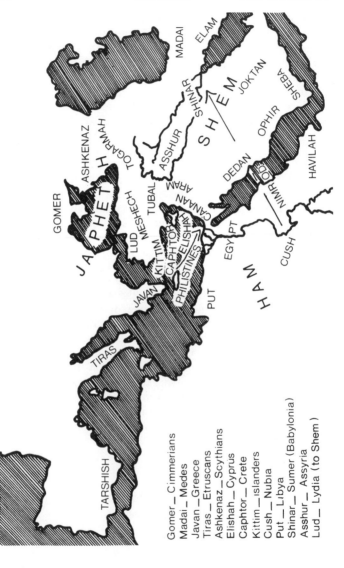

Gomer — Cimmerians
Madai — Medes
Javan — Greece
Tiras — Etruscans
Ashkenaz — Scythians
Elishah — Cyprus
Caphtor — Crete
Kittim — islanders
Cush — Nubia
Put — Libya
Shinar — Sumer (Babylonia)
Asshur — Assyria
Lud — Lydia (to Shem)

their father with a garment. As a result of this shameful little scene no blame is attached to Noah, but instead Noah curses Ham in the person of his son Canaan, and promises Shem and Japheth a great future.

As we find from the table of the nations in the next chapter, Shem stands for the Semitic peoples to the east of Palestine among whom the Hebrews themselves originated, Japheth for the nations to the north and west of Palestine, and Ham for the peoples of Africa, nearest being the Egyptians and beyond them the black races to their south (see the map on Fig. 3). From an ethnic point of view there are several inaccuracies in the groupings. Elam, for instance, is a son of Shem. But the Elamites, who lived in the present-day Iran or Persia, were not Semites by race. But by far the grossest deceit is the classification of the Canaanites with the nations of Africa. The Canaanites were as Semitic as the Hebrews, living in the same land and speaking the same Semitic dialect.

But, of course, the Canaanites were also the mortal enemies of the Hebrews at the time they invaded Palestine, and for many generations thereafter as each struggled for domination of the area. Here undoubtedly is the source of the curse on Canaan in the story. It reflects the bitter hatred engendered in the wars of conquest, and it reflects the threat which Canaanite religion with its sexual emphasis (see commentary on 1:26–31, *Male and female*) presented to the purity of Israel's faith.

But do that hatred and that threat justify a solemn curse in the Hebrew Scriptures? I for one have no hesitation in answering, No! For how was their paganism worse than the paganism of the other Semitic peoples and the peoples of the north who are blessed?

## THOUGHTS ON THE HEBREW TABLE OF THE NATIONS II

Genesis 9:20–29; 10:1–32 *(cont'd)*

(iii)

The distasteful story of the curse on Canaan ought not to be in the Bible. It speaks not of God's will but of Israel's exclusivism. There is not a long way to go from it to the extreme Zionism of the present day, whether in its Jewish or its Christian form, which is so concerned with the right of the Jews to be in the Holy Land that it completely forgets that the Arabs who live in the same land have their rights too. (It goes without saying that the Arabs are equally guilty in their attitude, but it is not their Scriptures we are studying.) And in so far as the curse involves Ham, it has its present-day equivalent in the hateful doctrines of white supremacy and apartheid, which many so-called Christians in the southern states of the U.S.A. and in South Africa think were ordained by God. Indeed, this passage has often figured prominently in their propaganda.

It would be difficult to think of two more obnoxious uses of Scripture than these, which seek to justify the modern racialism of (some) Christians and Jews by appealing to ancient Hebrew racialism.

But on second thoughts, perhaps the story ought to be kept after all. It may have got into Scripture because of the prejudice of the author and the Hebrews whom he was addressing. But in so far as it shows us not simply humanity in general but God's own people giving way to hatred and viciousness, it illustrates in a particularly apt way the parlous state of the world which God has to save. It was not the author's intention to expose the hypocrisy and partiality which can insinuate themselves even into the citadel of God. But under the guidance of the Holy Spirit that is the message which the story of the curse on Canaan now preaches.

### (iv)

Historically, the enslavement of Canaan which the curse looked forward to is probably the eventual victory of the Hebrew tribes over them after the Settlement. Similarly the reference to Japheth dwelling in the tents of Shem and in his turn enslaving Canaan may reflect the coming of the Philistines, an Indo-European people who arrived from the north in the Palestinian region about the same time as the Hebrews arrived from the

desert. Or it may refer to the Hittites of Asia Minor, though we
have no evidence that they ever invaded Palestine.

It is *not* to be taken, as some Christians have taken it, as
forecasting the gathering of the Gentiles into the Church and
the triumph of Christianity in Europe. That is not so offensive
an interpretation as the one attached by some modern Christians to the curse on Canaan. But it still smacks a little too much
of western (and white) superiority for my liking. And it doesn't
even have the excuse of being tied in with anything that the
original audience had any knowledge of. (Incidentally, if the
"blessing" on Japheth refers to the Philistines, then it must have
been current before they attacked Israel, for the Hebrews would
hardly have countenanced it after that. Possibly the piece in
brackets about the Philistines in 10:14 is a later attempt to
classify them among the Hamites.)

(v)

The only other detail I wish to consider in this commentary is
the little note about Nimrod, the first on earth to become a
warrior, and a "mighty hunter before the Lord" (10:8–9). Again
we do not know what the full story may have contained, but his
exploits in conquering many cities were clearly considerable. In
the sombre context of these chapters Nimrod emerges as the
world's first imperialist, the forerunner of many cruel empires
down the ages which have enslaved men and women by brute
force of arms for the greater glory of some cause or other. The
phrase "before the Lord" carries the suggestion not that God
approved of what he did, but that in his providence he permitted it.

(vi)

For further information about the peoples and places mentioned in Chapter 10 readers may consult one of the larger
Commentaries on Genesis or a Biblical Dictionary. I have only
one final comment. One of the reasons why these lists are in the
Bible was surely to remind Israel that she was by no means the
first or the greatest nation on earth. She was surrounded by

many larger and more accomplished peoples, who in God's providence were allowed their hour on the world's stage. Yet it was not them but Israel that he chose. The table in its hidden way has quite a lot to say about God's grace and about his opinion of what the world calls greatness.

## THE BABYLONIAN TOWER OF BABEL

Genesis 11:1-9

Now the whole earth had one language and few words. And as men migrated from the east, they found a plain in the land of Shinar and settled there. And they said to one another, "Come, let us make bricks, and burn them thoroughly." And they had brick for stone, and bitumen for mortar. Then they said, "Come, let us build ourselves a city, and a tower with its top in the heavens, and let us make a name for ourselves, lest we be scattered abroad upon the face of the whole earth." And the Lord came down to see the city and the tower, which the sons of men had built. And the Lord said, "Behold, they are one people, and they have all one language; and this is only the beginning of what they will do; and nothing that they propose to do will now be impossible for them. Come, let us go down, and there confuse their language, that they may not understand one another's speech." So the Lord scattered them abroad from there over the face of all the earth, and they left off building the city. Therefore its name was called Babel, because there the Lord confused the language of all the earth; and from there the Lord scattered them abroad over the face of all the earth.

This story doubtless also figured in Israel's old epic cycle, though with its Babylonian background there may be a Meso-potamian story behind it. At its simplest level it seems to offer an explanation of the origin of language, the skill which above all marks human beings off from the animals, but which because of the variety of tongues at the same time erects such high barriers between them. It is a subject which must have given ancient peoples much food for thought, and there are tales from many parts of the world which like the story in Genesis trace the bewildering diversity of languages back to a decision of the gods to confound an original single language which all the first "men" spoke.

(i)

Typically, however, in Hebrew hands this motif becomes the starting point not of a sermon on fate but of a sermon on sin. In the Hebrew story God confounds the language of "men" not out of pique but because they built the Tower of Babel.

It is in this part of the story that the Babylonian background is most evident. For the Tower of Babel can only be a *ziggurat,* the name given to the great sacred towers of Mesopotamian religion which were set up near a god's temple. From archaeological excavations and contemporary documents we have a good idea of what these *ziggurats* looked like. They were huge structures, usually square but sometimes rectangular, consisting of several storeys, the size of each storey being less than the one below it. Staircases or ramps were attached to the sides for access up and down. It is probable but not certain that a small shrine was built on top.

A difficult cuneiform tablet from Uruk (the Erech of Gen. 10:10), dated to the third century B.C., gives the following measurements for one such *ziggurat* (length by width by height in feet):

> First storey: 295 by 295 by 108
> Second storey: 256 by 256 by 59
> Third storey: 197 by 197 by 19.75
> Fourth storey: 167.5 by 167.5 by 19.75
> Fifth storey: 138 by 138 by 19.75
> Sixth storey: 108.5 by 108.5 by 19.75
> Seventh storey: 79 by 79 by 49

If the seven heights are added it will be found that the total height (295 feet) was the same as the length and width at ground level.

It is not unlikely that this tablet in fact describes the *ziggurat* of Babylon, though as it was at a later period than when the Hebrew story was composed. The ground remains of this *ziggurat* along with part of its first staircase were uncovered in excavations at Babylon adjacent to the great temple of Marduk, and measure 298 feet square, which is as near to the specifications of the tablet as makes no difference. See the sketch (Fig. 4) for a rough reconstruction.

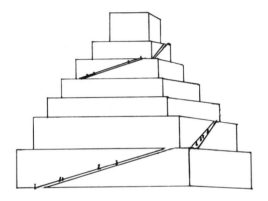

(ii)

The temple of Marduk at Babylon was called *Esagil* meaning "the great house", and its *ziggurat* was called *Etemenanki* meaning "the house of the foundation of heaven and earth". Like the Temple at Jerusalem *Esagil* was primarily regarded as the home of the deity, where he dwelt when on earth and where he could be approached. Unlike our modern church buildings, only the priests entered it, the people worshipping outside in the courtyard. In line with this the *ziggurat* must have been thought of not so much as a means by which the Babylonians could take themselves nearer their god, but as a means by which the god's route to earth and to them was made easier, the shrine on the top being a kind of "staging-post" or "half-way house". Similarly Marduk's city *Bab-ili* "the gate of the god" (or sometimes *Bab-ilani* "the gate of the gods") must have got its name because it was there that he had his temple and his tower and chose to make himself available to his people.

The reasoning of the Babylonians may not unfairly be compared with Jacob's when, waking from his dream at Bethel, he said, "This is none other than the *house of God* [Hebrew *Beth-el*] and this is the *gate of heaven"* (Gen. 28:17). Indeed it is not impossible that Jacob's acquaintance with the *ziggurats* of Mesopotamia was the basis of his vision of a ladder (or staircase) set up on earth whose "top" reached to "the heavens" (verse 12). See verse 4 in Chapter 11.

### (iii)

Any Babylonian story behind the Hebrew story must then have had a *positive* purpose, to celebrate in genuine awe and humility the foundation of the greatest city on earth and the establishing of an unbreakable chain linking it with heaven and with Marduk, the King of the gods. It would be most unlikely to have had any reference to the origin of language.

It is possible that there are hidden allusions to such a story in some of the building inscriptions of later Babylonian kings who repaired or renovated the temple and its *ziggurat.* Here is what Nabopolassar says in the seventh century B.C. (he was the father of the famous Nebuchadnezzar);

> The lord Marduk commanded me concerning *Etemenanki,* the staged tower of Babylon, which before my time had become dilapidated and ruinous, that I should make its foundation secure in the bosom of the nether world, and make its summit like the heavens . . . I caused baked bricks to be made . . . I caused streams of bitumen to be brought . . . I myself measured the dimensions . . . For my lord Marduk I bowed my neck, I took off my robe, the sign of my royal blood, and on my head I bore bricks and earth. As for Nebuchadnezzar my firstborn son, the beloved of my heart, I made him bear the mortar, the offerings of wine and oil, in company with my subjects.
>
> (translation by A. Parrot)

Note the baked bricks and the bitumen for mortar as in Gen. 11 (these were not Palestinian building materials), and above all note the idea of making the summit as high as the heavens. Note too the king's personal involvement in the proceedings. It is as if

he were presiding at a re-enactment of the first solemn construction of the great tower as handed down in his people's legends.

## THE HEBREW TOWER OF BABEL

Genesis 11:1–9 (*cont'd*)

### (iv)

The Hebrew story-teller stands this Babylonian story on its
head. What had been a tale of a people's religious devotion
becomes a tale of humanity's pride once again going too far and
once again drawing disaster in its wake.

It will be remembered that Shinar (verse 2) was where
Nimrod, the "mighty hunter" and the world's first warrior,
performed his conquering exploits (10:8ff.). Shinar is probably
the Hebrew equivalent of Sumer, the land of the Sumerians, the
predecessors of the Babylonians. It looks very much as if the
story of the tower is meant to carry on the symbolism of the
story of Nimrod. The history of Mesopotamia, the earliest
centre of human civilization, is being presented as the climax of
the long and dreadful catalogue of "man's" crimes which began
with Adam's "first disobedience" in the garden. And encapsu-
lating that history is the decision of its earliest inhabitants (note
how they come from the East, where the garden was and where
Cain had been condemned to wander—see 2:8 and 4:16) to
build the Tower of Babel.

### (v)

It is at this point that the author works in the language motif
which he had probably got from some other old pagan tale. As a
punishment for building the tower he has God confounding the
participants' language and scattering them over the whole
earth, so creating the situation of diverse and hostile nationali-
ties and races which was summarized in the tables of Chapter
10.

His story is a short one, but it is beautifully structured. This is
seen from the following equations between its two halves:

| | |
|---|---|
| *the whole earth* (verse 1) | *all the earth* (verses 8 and 9) |
| *they said to one another* (verse 3) | *one another's speech* (verse 7) |
| *they said, Come* (verse 4) | *the Lord said, Come* (verse 7) |
| *let us build a city* (verse 4) | *they left off building the city* (verse 8) |
| *let us make a name for ourselves* (verse 4) | *its name was called* (verse 9) |
| *lest we be scattered* (verse 4) | *the Lord scattered them* (verses 8 and 9) |

Yet in its main connection it positively creaks. For the link between the story of the tower and the confusion of tongues involves a play on words which every Hebrew would immediately recognize as false. The audience must have known that *Babel*, the Hebrew equivalent of the Babylonian *Babili*, meant "gate of the god". The phrase used by Jacob in 28:17, "this is the gate of heaven", shows that. Yet the author is asking them to believe that it meant "confusion". The Hebrew verb for "confound" is *balal* which repeats the *l* but has only one *b*, whereas in *Babel* the *b* is repeated and there is only one *l*.

It is apparent from this fictional etymology that the author is not really interested in the origin of languages as such, any more than he had been in what the Babylonians thought about their own tower.

(vi)

He is directing us to a much deeper level of meaning. His ultimate concern is not with the Babylonians and their tower, nor is it with people's inability to understand one another's languages. It is with all human beings and with their inability to live in harmony with their fellows at all. In the story this disunity is God's doing, but that is only in the story. In reality human beings have brought their divisions on themselves, and they have done so because they have first made a division between themselves and God.

With this little parable the wheel of Genesis' first eleven chapters has come round full circle. And at the end as all through these chapters we have the same paradoxical juxtaposition of humanity's successes and humanity's failures. Like human knowledge and human sin they are inseparable. The modern view of "man" is not unaware of the dark side to his nature, but in the last analysis it treats it lightly and is euphorically optimistic about his prospects. These ancient chapters take exactly the opposite view.

With their "knowledge of good and evil" human beings have indeed got hold of "godlike" power, and as a result they can put down to their credit many "godlike" achievements. But their trouble is that they do not know when to call a halt. Their desire for more and more knowledge is insatiable, their lust for more and more power never assuaged. And here finally they are storming the heights of heaven itself and seeking to drive God from his throne. In thus overreaching themselves they have condemned the world to discord and grief as now not only individual opposes individual, but nation opposes nation and race opposes race, and peace and brotherhood have fled the earth. Their greatest act of united zeal has been typically a bid to free themselves from God. Typically it has ended with a humanity more split and fractured than ever.

Eden has changed into Babel. The "delight" of the world God created has become the "confusion" of the world "man" has created for himself.

## TOWARDS THE FUTURE

Genesis 11:10–32

These are the descendants of Shem. When Shem was a hundred years old, he became the father of Arpachshad two years after the flood; and Shem lived after the birth of Arpachshad five hundred years, and had other sons and daughters.

When Arpachshad had lived thirty-five years, he became the father of Shelah; and Arpachshad lived after the birth of Shelah four hundred and three years, and had other sons and daughters.

When Shelah had lived thirty years, he became the father of Eber; and Shelah lived after the birth of Eber four hundred and three years, and had other sons and daughters.

When Eber had lived thirty-four years, he became the father of Peleg; and Eber lived after the birth of Peleg four hundred and thirty years, and had other sons and daughters.

When Peleg had lived thirty years, he became the father of Reu; and Peleg lived after the birth of Reu two hundred and nine years, and had other sons and daughters.

When Reu had lived thirty-two years, he became the father of Serug; and Reu lived after the birth of Serug two hundred and seven years, and had other sons and daughters.

When Serug had lived thirty years, he became the father of Nahor; and Serug lived after the birth of Nahor two hundred years, and had other sons and daughters.

When Nahor had lived twenty-nine years, he became the father of Terah; and Nahor lived after the birth of Terah a hundred and nineteen years, and had other sons and daughters.

When Terah had lived seventy years, he became the father of Abram, Nahor, and Haran.

Now these are the descendants of Terah. Terah was the father of Abram, Nahor, and Haran; and Haran was the father of Lot. Haran died before his father Terah in the land of his birth, in Ur of the Chaldeans. And Abram and Nahor took wives; the name of Abram's wife was Sarai, and the name of Nahor's wife, Milcah, the daughter of Haran the father of Milcah and Iscah. Now Sarai was barren; she had no child.

Terah took Abram his son and Lot the son of Haran, his grandson, and Sarai his daughter-in-law, his son Abram's wife, and they went forth together from Ur of the Chaldeans to go into the land of Canaan; but when they came to Haran, they settled there. The days of Terah were two hundred and five years; and Terah died in Haran.

Our eleven chapters conclude with a more detailed genealogy of the Semites which gradually narrows down to the tribes of Upper Mesopotamia around Haran (in the language of Mesopotamia Harran), an area with which in the rest of Genesis the Hebrew Patriarchs had the closest of contacts. It was there that in Chapter 24 Abraham sent his servant to procure a wife for Isaac, and it was there that Jacob fled to escape the wrath of Esau and there that he also found his wife. The Patriarchs were the chiefs of semi-nomadic clans who moved about on the fringes of the settled lands around the so-called "Fertile Crescent" (see the map on Fig. 2). But if anywhere could be called their "home", it was that area in the north. However, they seem to have journeyed from time to time to the richer regions of Babylonia, and it is at Ur of the Chaldees (AV) that we find Terah and his clan as Chapter 11 finishes.

(i)

It is wrong to think of the Terahites as citizens of Ur, which was after Babylon itself probably the most splendid representative of Mesopotamian culture and civilization in the Patriarchal period. They would be more likely to have lived in encampments outside its walls and entered it as occasion demanded to trade and barter. Nevertheless, it is symbolically most appropriate that the history of God's own people should begin in such a city, in the region of the ancient world which was at the time the grandest and most powerful of all, the region where Nimrod the warrior had settled and where the inhabitants had built the Tower of Babel to join earth to heaven. By quitting it and returning to his own folk at Harran, Terah by implication condemns it and all it stood for.

He is taking the first step on that greater journey which his son Abraham will continue, when in faith and in answer to God's call he in turn abandons the Patriarchal homeland, not to go back to the great city of Ur, but to go forward looking for a city "which has foundations, whose builder and maker is God" (Heb. 11:10).

(ii)

We end our commentary then with a glimmer of hope amid the encircling gloom of the world's sin.

The main thrust of the eleven chapters has been negative as they have portrayed sin spreading like a virus and infecting mortally not only humanity but the very physical Creation. And in the background there has now and again been glimpsed a larger force of evil bolstering up the sin of "man". There has been a positive side as well, but once his great work in creating the universe was past, it has been a story not of God defeating sin and evil but of him sadly containing it, not of him saving "men" but of him with a heavy heart preventing them from quite bringing about the destruction of all that he had made and planned. We could almost call it a rearguard action as desperately he defends his Kingdom against their usurping hands.

But now at last, just as the eleventh chapter draws to a close—indeed just as the eleventh hour is striking—God launches his counter-offensive. He begins his attempt to reclaim the kingdom which "men" thought they had filched from him. The call to Abraham which will set the Gospel story in motion is about to be issued. It will be a long time before Israel reaches her Promised Land. It will be longer still before, constructing his own staircase between heaven and earth, God comes down again to Babel and in the person of his Son wins his decisive victory over sin and evil. But he has now found a few faithful souls who acknowledge him and not themselves as King, and through them and their seed his Kingdom shall one day fill the world.

## FURTHER READING

Books marked * are more suitable for initial study

Commentaries:
  U. Cassuto, *A Commentary on the Book of Genesis* (Magnes Press and Oxford University Press)
      I *From Adam to Noah* (1961)
      II *From Noah to Abraham* (1964)
*R. Davidson, *Genesis 1–11* (The Cambridge Bible Commentary on the New English Bible) (Cambridge University Press, 1973)
*D. Kidner, *Genesis: An Introduction and Commentary* (Tyndale Old Testament Commentaries) (Inter-Varsity Press, 1967)

G. von Rad, *Genesis,* Second Edition (Old Testament Library) (SCM Press and Westminster Press, 1963)

*A. Richardson, *Genesis 1–11, Introduction and Commentary* (Torch Bible Commentaries) (SCM Press, 1953)

J. Skinner, *A Critical and Exegetical Commentary on Genesis,* Second Edition (The International Critical Commentary) (T. and T. Clark, 1930)

E. A. Speiser, *Genesis: Introduction, Translation and Notes* (Anchor Bible) (Doubleday, 1964)

B. Vawter, *On Genesis: A New Reading* (Geoffrey Chapman, 1977)

Other Studies:

W. Beyerlin (editor), *Near Eastern Religious Texts relating to the Old Testament* (Old Testament Library) (SCM Press and Westminster Press, 1978)

N. C. Habel, *Literary Criticism of the Old Testament* (Guides to Biblical Scholarship, Old Testament Series) (Fortress Press, 1971)

S. McEvenue, S. J., *The Narrative Style of the Priestly Writer* (Biblical Institute Press, Rome, 1971)

*A. Parrot, *The Flood and Noah's Ark* (Studies in Biblical Archaeology No.1) (SCM Press, 1955)

*A. Parrot, *The Tower of Babel* (Studies in Biblical Archaeology No.2) (SCM Press, 1955)

*S. Sandmel, *The Enjoyment of Scripture: The Law, the Prophets, and the Writings* (Oxford University Press, New York, 1972), especially Chapter IV, "The Pentateuch"

W. Vischer, *The Witness of the Old Testament to Christ,* Volume I, *The Pentateuch* (Lutterworth Press, 1949)

*C. Westermann, *Creation* (SPCK and Fortress Press, 1974)